Stuart Hylton

THE LITTLE BOOK OF THE
1950s

Illustrated by Lucy Simpkin

First published 2013

The History Press
The Mill, Brimscombe Port
Stroud, Gloucestershire, GL5 2QG
www.thehistorypress.co.uk

© Stuart Hylton, 2013

The right of Stuart Hylton to be identified as the Author
of this work has been asserted in accordance with the
Copyright, Designs and Patents Act 1988.

British Library Cataloguing in Publication Data.
A catalogue record for this book is available from the British Library.

ISBN 978 0 7524 8858 5

Typesetting and origination by The History Press
Printed in Great Britain

Contents

Acknowledgements

I have a hundred and one sources to whom I am indebted for the material in this book. I am not allowed the space to acknowledge them all and it would be invidious for me to mention just a select few and omit others. So I will. In no paticular order: Asa Briggs' *History of Broadcasting (volume 5)* throws much light on the mysterious world of the pre-competition BBC. David Kynaston's books *Austerity Britain* and *Family Britain* give a wonderful overview of the decade and the post-war lead-up to it. The Oxford Dictionary of Space Exploration provided a wealth of information for the space race chapter. I can also recommend Peter Hennesy's *Having it So Good: Britain in the 1950s*, Dominic Sandbrook's *Never Had it So Good*, Peter Lewis' *The 1950s*, and Akhtar and Humphries' *The Fifties and Sixties – A Lifestyle Revolution*. But the simplest thing is to Google any subject that takes your fancy in the book and be prepared to be amazed at the wealth of information that is out there on it – some of it even accurate! I apologise to and thank the many sources I was not able to acknowledge. And, of course, modesty prevents me mentioning my own small contribution to the topic – *From Rationing to Rock*.

Introduction

For some people, the 1950s was simply the time they lived in whilst waiting for the swinging sixties to begin. However, for me they provide a fascinating hinge between the past and the present. Many of the features we take for granted as part of modern life, from widespread home and car ownership, to jet travel, rock and roll, the discovery of teenagers as a separate species, the moral codes to which society – sometimes reluctantly or imperfectly – still adheres today, right through to the idea of space travel as something more than the subject of comic-book fantasy, had their origins in the 1950s.

It was also the decade in which the nation started to shed some of the delusions of grandeur that it had entertained right up until the end of the Second World War and beyond. British ideas of being a world superpower and global police officer were put well and truly into context, as efforts to secure the Suez Canal met with ignominious defeat; most of our Empire inexplicably developed the idea that they might prefer to be independent, rather than continue being colonised by us. Upstart nations like Germany and Japan started having economic miracles, despite having lost the war and – Good Heavens – the United States even beat us at football!

It was not all bad news. We had the Festival of Britain to give a war-weary nation a pat on the back, the Coronation, uniting us behind a new monarch, and a hundred and one smaller steps towards making our lives more convenient, more exciting and more varied.

This is not a learned history of the decade. Others have already covered that ground admirably. This is a book for you to dip in and out of, as the mood takes you. You will find it populated with a rich assortment of villains, protesters and extravagant characters; you will see ideas and inventions, which we today take as commonplace, as they first emerge, and attitudes that you may have thought vanished with Queen Victoria. As American senator Jesse Helms almost once said, I may not know much about history, but I know what I like. I hope you enjoy.

Stuart Hylton, 2013

Let Me Entertain You …
Broadcasting 1950s-Style

Television in its infancy

Whatever the choice of family entertainment you will find it
in TELEVISION. It has brought a new meaning into home life
and thousands who used to seek their entertainment outside,
now find their television set a source of untold pleasure at
home. Why not learn more about it?

(1950s advertisement for the new wonder of the age)

The 1950s was the decade in which television came of age. First,
and foremost, there was the dramatic increase in television set
ownership. When broadcasting
resumed after the war, there were
just 20,000 television sets, generally
belonging to people living within
30 miles of the British Broadcasting
Corporation's (BBC's) only
transmitter at Alexandra Palace. As
late as 1949, the majority of households
had never seen a set in action, let alone
owned one. Nonetheless, the potential
market for television could
already be seen – set
ownership had already
reached over 100,000 by
the end of the forties. In

1950, the BBC opened what it boasted was the world's most advanced transmitter at Sutton Coldfield, opening up the joys of viewing to an entirely new region. Set ownership took another leap, to 343,882, by March of that year. King George's funeral, the coronation and the coming of commercial television helped swell the numbers to around 2 million by 1953 and 4 million two years later. The number of combined TV and radio licences exceeded those for radio alone for the first time in 1957, and by the end of the decade, 10.5 million television licences were being issued – 72 per cent of all households had a set.

Despite being monopoly holders of the national television franchise, many at the top of the BBC in the early 1950s took a very dim view of the upstart service. In their view:
' … it was not a medium to be taken seriously: pantomime horses and chorus girls were its natural ingredients; it was not suitable for news or current affairs.'

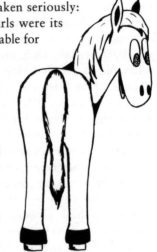

Worse still, it could have a toxic effect on broadcasting as a whole:
' … the high purposes of the Corporation would be trivialised by the influence of those concerned with what could be transmitted in visual terms.'

Accordingly, in 1950, the Corporation set up a 2,500-strong Television Panel, with the remit of

helping the BBC to deliver: '... a keener, more sensitive and more intelligent appreciation on the part of all who see it of the world about us.'

(This from the organisation that would shortly give us *Bill and Ben the Flowerpot Men*). Television was thus starved of both cash and influence within the Corporation. In 1947, the total budget for television broadcasting was just £716,666, compared with the £6,556,293 allocated for radio, and had reached only £3 million by 1951. Prior to 1950, television was not even represented on the Corporation's Board and thereafter its appointed champion was the Director of the Spoken Word (who does not sound like a pictures man). In 1956, a Director of Television was finally appointed, but Gerald Beadle did not own a set and saw the post as a means of winding down towards retirement.

At the same time as believing that television was a medium of no importance, officials at the BBC were also afraid that it would turn us into a nation of square-eyed couch potatoes. Modern viewers would find few grounds for such a fear with broadcasting as it was in 1950 – limited to just 30 hours a week. Programmes would start at 3 p.m. on a weekday (5 p.m. on Sundays) and would stop between 6 and 7 p.m., to enable parents to prise small children away from the set and get them to bed, and for older children to do their homework. Transmissions would normally close down entirely by 10.30 p.m. It was not until 1955 that the permitted hours of broadcasting increased to forty per week.

The battle over commercial television

At the start of the fifties, the BBC had a monopoly hold over all types of broadcasting. The values of Lord Reith, the pre-war Director General, still held sway in the corridors of Broadcasting House and the nation was given a diet of worthy, but often dull, programming. The arrival of a post-war Conservative Government under Churchill, in 1951, was the beginning of the end of the monopoly; Churchill had hated the BBC since the days of the 1926 General Strike, when he had tried to take it over as a propaganda tool. He regarded the Corporation as a nest of socialists, or worse. A White Paper was commissioned, which recommended licensing a new commercial television channel.

The nation was deeply divided on the subject; the case for keeping the BBC's monopoly was advanced by the National Television Council, while the calls for a commercial alternative were led by the Popular Television Association. Each side recruited celebrities and other people of influence to their cause, and some rather overblown cases were made for them, particularly by the pro-monopolists. One of the leading voices for them was, of course, Lord Reith himself. Never one given to over-statement, he likened the influence of commercial television to smallpox, the bubonic plague and dog racing, and made a somewhat patronising comment to television's growing audience. Easier hire purchase, he said, had enabled more poor people to acquire television sets, and Parliament had a grave responsibility to these people, to stop television becoming a by-word for crude and trivial entertainment. Meanwhile, Conservative politician, Lord Hailsham, likened the battle over commercial television to that of the nation's survival in the Second World War. In those days, he said, the BBC had been the voice of freedom, and it was now in danger of handing over the greatest instrument for good that had been devised since the printing press, to purely commercial interests.

As we now know, the anti-monopolists won the day, and commercial television started broadcasting in the London area in September 1955. The parliamentary act authorising the new channels included a duty on them to 'inform' and 'educate' as well as 'entertain', but (no doubt prompted by the need to build audience share and advertising revenue) the new commercial interests were – or soon became – unashamedly populist. They would give the public what they wanted, not what some higher authority thought was good for them. (According to one ITV executive, the public wanted to see girls, wrestling, bright musicals, quiz shows and real-life dramas). They also had a much larger budget for programming than BBC TV, and were able to poach many of the BBC's staff. Small wonder, then, that by the end of 1957, they had secured a 72 per cent audience share and were well on the way to becoming that infamous licence to print money.

Even after its establishment, a number of interests (including the Labour Party, some newspapers, senior clergy and academics) continued to lobby for commercial television to be closed down. The *Spectator* called commercial broadcasting 'a monument to fraud and a daily reminder of the worthlessness of political promises', and the *Daily Express* carried a leader in January 1956 calling for the authorities 'to write off ITV as an experiment that went wrong and hand the wavelength over to the BBC before it got completely out of control'.

One of the interesting aspects of BBC programming during its monopoly years was its desperate desire not to abuse its prominence by seeming to be partisan, as seen in the fourteen-day rule, which forbade any matter due to be discussed in Parliament in the next fourteen days to be discussed on television. This was naturally something of a constraint on current affairs broadcasting and, by the mid-1950s, had become an obvious absurdity. Things came to a head in February 1955, when the programme *In the News*, one of the Corporation's few attempts to be hard-hitting over current affairs, was stopped from discussing atomic bomb testing. The programme's panel decided they would no longer be bound by the rule – which was simply a convention, rather than anything binding and statutory. The Postmaster General (the Minister responsible for television) tried to enforce it, but found he had no legal basis for doing so. This, and a media campaign, forced him to back down.

The BBC's approach to television news was similarly blinkered. Until commercial competition forced them to review their approach, their newsreaders were not trusted to script their own reports, the names of the newsreaders were not announced to the viewers and their faces were not even seen (caption cards being shown on the screen instead). The only visual interest tended to come from cinema-style newsreels, which might be several days out of date. As Robin Day said: 'Independent Television News set new standards for vigour, enterprise and pace for television news, making the BBC version look stiff and stuffy.'

What were we watching?

'Television is a very unusual business. You don't necessarily make more money in television if you provide a better product.'
(Sidney Bernstein, Head of Granada Television)

Here is a small sample of the treats in store for the 1950s television viewer.

When we were very young ...
If you were very young, or had young children, from April 1952 you were likely to tune in to *Watch with Mother*, broadcast from 3.45–4.00 p.m., between the midday nap and when the older children were getting back from school. Among its attractions were:

Andy Pandy (first shown in 1950) – a puppet whose taste in clothing would get him bullied at any modern school, and who lived in a picnic basket with a teddy bear, and a rag doll called Looby Loo. The programme always ended with the song 'Time to go home ... Andy is waving goodbye'.

Bill and Ben the Flower Pot Men (1952) – with its cliffhanger ending of 'was it Bill or was it Ben' who had committed this episode's naughtiness? Readers may be interested to know that Bill and Ben had their real-life origins in William and Benjamin Brabban, the naughty younger brothers of the show's creator.

Rag, Tag and Bobtail (1953) – featuring the glove puppets Rag, a hedgehog, Tag, a mouse, and Bobtail, a rabbit.

The Woodentops (1955) – a family of wooden dolls who lived on a farm with Buttercup the cow, Spotty Dog and domestic help in the form of Mr and Mrs Scrubbitt.

Watch with Mother would run until 1973.

Home on the range
For the older children there was a steady transatlantic supply of cowboys.

The Lone Ranger (who was not actually alone, but always accompanied by his faithful, Native American sidekick, Tonto). He was supposed to be an ex-Texas Ranger who went around righting wrongs on his white horse, Silver. He fired silver bullets and shouted 'Hi-yo Silver, away!' quite a lot. Deeply conscious of his duties as a role model to his younger viewers, the Lone Ranger taught the tiny tots to speak with perfect grammar and never shoot-to-kill.

The Cisco Kid and his companion, Pancho, were originally outlaws wanted for some unspecified crime, but went around performing Robin Hood-type services for the poor and oppressed. A similar role was assigned to the character Hopalong Cassidy.

Roy Rogers, with his golden palomino horse, Trigger, and his golden palomino wife, Dale Evans was famous for being the most heavily merchandised individual in Hollywood, after Walt Disney.

There were also home-produced, non-cowboy heroes. The novel *Ivanhoe* was published in 1820 and was written by Sir Walter Scott. It was about a knight in twelfth-century England, and when adapted for the screen, it provided an early outing for future James Bond, Roger Moore in the title role.

Robin Hood (feared by the bad, loved by the good) provided an opportunity for Richard Greene to run through cardboard forests, outwitting the wicked Sheriff of Nottingham.

From November 1958 onwards, children wanting non-fictional television could tune into *Blue Peter*, hosted by a former Miss Great Britain, Leila Williams and actor Christopher Trace, and which promised 'toys, model railways, games, stories and cartoons'. The name comes from the flag flown by a ship about to embark on a voyage of adventure. The show's original puppy died after making its first television appearance, sending researchers scurrying to the pet shop for a look-alike, which became known, after a viewer's poll, as 'Petra'. This purchase, and her upkeep, would have consumed a substantial part of the programme's budget, which was initially just £180 per show.

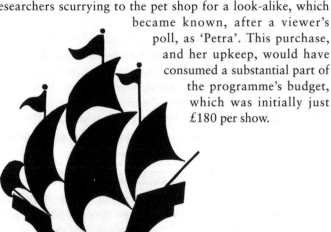

Then there was *Crackerjack*, a series of children's variety shows originally hosted by Aemonn Andrews that ran from 1955 to 1984. Among its defining features was the quiz game Double or Drop, in which contestants were given a prize for a correct answer and a cabbage for each wrong one.

Drop any of your armful and you were 'out'. There were also opportunities to cover a celebrity in gunge. The youthful audience were encouraged to shout 'Crackerjack!' should the presenter ever utter the word, and it gave the world such catch-phrases as 'It's Friday, it's five o'clock, it's Crackerjack!' and (shockingly for a 1950s BBC children's programme) 'Don't get your knickers in a twist!'

Grown-ups could watch things like Phil Silvers as the devious Sergeant Bilko, carrying out his latest money making scam, or, for domestic comedy, there were the scatter-brained antics of *I Love Lucy* and her bandleader husband, Desi Arnaz. By the end of 1956, the two television channels were showing, or had shown, no less than twelve different American comedy series. However, not all of the most popular 1950s shows for adults or children were American imports.

Evening all

The character Police Constable George Dixon first made his appearance in the 1950s film *The Blue Lamp*, in the course of which he was shot dead by a young gangster – not the most promising start to a role on which a career could be built, you might think. But five years later, through the miraculous healing powers of television, George Dixon was resurrected when the television series *Dixon of Dock Green* was launched. It would run from 1955 to 1976. Dixon (or rather the actor Jack Warner, who played him) was already sixty years old when the series started – a little mature to be pounding the beat – but he continued, thanks to a series of increasingly sedentary roles in the police station, and by stretching the audience's credulity ever further, only 'retiring' from the force when aged over eighty. No matter, by 1961 the series, written by Ted Willis, was the nation's second most popular television show, attracting an audience of 13.85 million. It was only as the grittier and more realistic cop shows – like *Z Cars* – began to air that Dixon's ratings started to slip, for gritty and realistic *Dixon of Dock Green* was not.

Supposedly set in the East End of London (which in real life was, by this time, the stamping ground of the Kray twins and their like) Dixon's police station seemed to deal with nothing much more than petty crime and the home lives of the police officers. You always felt as if the show's villains were the sort who, when apprehended, would shake the arresting officer by the hand and say, 'It's a fair cop, Constable, you've got me bang to rights.' Confronted by the real Kray twins, George Dixon would have sorted them out with a good talking to and a clip round the ear. But only once.

Hancock's Half Hour

Hancock's Half Hour was one of a number of 1950s shows that made the transition from radio to television, with the two series running together for some time. It was written by Ray Galton and Alan Simpson, and was an important influence in the development of the situation comedy. It moved away from the music-hall variety theatre approach of quick-fire gag cracking interspersed with music, towards the idea of a single continuous narrative in which character development was as important as free-standing punchlines.

Hancock played a down-at-heel version of himself – Anthony Aloysius St John Hancock – a largely unemployed actor/comedian residing at 23 Railway Cuttings, East Cheam. His principal support came from Sid James, his criminally inclined confidant.

The rest of the supporting cast for the radio series (first launched in November 1954) included an array of British comedy talent, such as Hattie Jacques, Moira Lister, Andree Melly, Hugh Lloyd, Dick Emery, John le Mesurier, Richard Wattis, Pat Coombs, Rolf Harris, Kenneth Williams and Bert Kwouk. The television version ran from 1956–61, and the final series focussed more on the man himself, with its title being shortened to *Hancock*. Sid James was dropped from the show because Hancock was afraid that they were starting to be seen as a double act. It was from this series that many of his classic episodes came – the 'Blood Donor', the 'Radio Ham', the 'Bowmans' and the 'Bedsitter' – and they stand in comparison, over fifty years later, with any comedy programme that has been offered since.

Get rich quick
Lovers of quiz shows were well catered for by the new commercial channel. Two of their most popular formats were transferred across from Radio Luxemburg. Hughie Green (a man once described as having all the sincerity of a clockwork ferret) compered *Double Your Money*, which had contestants answering questions for a cash prize that doubled each time – starting at £1 and soaring to a dizzying £32. Contestants could then enter the Treasure Trail that led all the way to a possible £1,000 prize.

Michael Miles' *Take Your Pick* featured the yes–no interlude, in which contestants were interrogated by Miles and had to reply without saying the words 'yes' or 'no' and being gonged out. They were then allowed to choose from a series of boxes, each containing prizes. Miles would try to get them to sell him the key to the box for cash, and the prize would turn out either to be something valuable, like a washing machine or a holiday, or a worthless booby prize.

The spice of life
One of the fears of the theatre was that television would kill variety, and nowhere was the competition more clear than in the case of *Sunday Night at the London Palladium*. Between 1955 and 1967 it was the flagship weekend show for the commercial channel – an estimated 20 million people saw Cliff

Richard and the Shadows play on it, and vicars rescheduled their church services, so that God did not clash with his rock and roll representative on earth. The first show aired in September 1955, the week commercial television opened, with Gracie Fields as its star. Other mainstream famous guests included Judy Garland and Bob Hope, as well as popular music favourites of the fifties, like Bill Haley and His Comets, Johnny Ray and Liberace. A performance by the Beatles in October 1963 gave the English media the term 'Beatlemania' (though others claim to have been its inventor). It was a traditional variety show and, as well as supporting acts, also featured a knockabout game show, called *Beat the Clock*, for the audience and the diversion of the high-kicking chorus girls the Tiller Girls.

All white on the night

Another (to modern audiences more questionable) form of light entertainment was *The Black and White Minstrel Show*, in which a group of blacked-up minstrels sung medleys of popular songs in a setting glamorised by a group of female dancers, called the Television Toppers. Unimaginable today, the show aired from 1959–78 and drew some of the highest viewing figures of any programme, winning the international Golden Rose of Montreux. Accusations of racism from the late 1960s onwards took many years to dent the show's popularity. Equally questionable in some eyes was the BBC's engagement with other European broadcasters, which gave us Eurovision and its misbegotten offspring, the *Eurovision Song Contest,* first held in 1956.

The theatre strikes back

One way the theatre tried to compete with the upstart competition was with filth. One not-untypical provincial theatre offered *The Revue Riot of the Year*, entitled 'We Couldn't Care Less' (only with the word 'care' deleted and replaced with 'wear'). The advertisements said 'Don't wonder if there are girls on the moon – come and see these "heavenly bodies"!' They promised 'The latest rage from the American strip shows, the "wriggle dance"' and asked, 'Would you prefer to live in the nude? We show you what it would be like'. Match that, BBC TV! Cinema attendances also suffered from the competition, and they fought back with wider screens (Cinerama, 1952, CinemaScope, 1953, and Todd-AO, 1956), brighter colour and lavish productions that television's budget and small screens could not match. They also had the added bonus of being in 3D.

On the radio - what were we listening to?

But enough of television. For much of the decade, radio was the pre-eminent broadcast medium, certainly in terms of audience size. Let us remind ourselves of a few of the favourite programmes of the day.

The Archers

In 1950, the BBC started broadcasting 'an everyday story of country folk' or, as someone put it, 'a farming Dick Barton'. The idea was to provide a soap opera with enough drama to hold the average listener's attention, while at the same time the Ministry of Agriculture could use it to transmit the latest agricultural efficiency hints to the real farming community. It made for some very clunky scripts, but, sixty years and 16,700 episodes later, *The Archers* is still going strong and has been polled as the most listened-to Radio 4 programme apart from the news. At its height, 60 per cent of the country's adult population listened in and when, in 1955, the BBC needed a spoiler to take the shine off the opening night of commercial television they looked, not to their own television channel, but to radio. That night, 9.4 million people listened as newlywed Grace Archer 'perished' in a fire at her stables, trying to rescue her horse. (Apparently, there was another motivation for writing her out of the series – the actress who played her was trying to get the rest of the cast to join a trade union. It was easier than having her killed in real life.)

The drama takes place in the village of Ambridge, in the fictional county of Borsetshire (which lies between Worcestershire and Warwickshire). A particular feature of the programme over the years has been the cameo appearances by famous people (everyone from royalty, such as Princess Margaret and the Duchess of Cornwall, to Dame Edna Everidge and more). It has even had the ultimate accolade of being parodied by Tony Hancock. In his version, *The Bowmans*, Hancock is an actor playing a rustic who gets written out of the series. When public demand forces the broadcasters to relent and reinstate him, he only agrees to do so if he is allowed to script the next episode. His revenge on the rest of the cast is suitably and hilariously terrible.

Some aficionados would say that the programme is not what it used to be. In the 'good old days', the village was populated by true rustics, whose horizons did not stretch beyond the nearby cathedral city of 'Felpersham', and whose idea of a cliffhanger was Walter Gabriel getting a touch of mange in his mangelwurzels (I may have given away my non-farming background here). Today, much of the village appears to have been populated by city slickers and other deviants, and you can scarcely tune in for people falling fatally off their rooves, committing crimes or engaging in forms of sexual activity that were positively illegal in the 1950s. Thank goodness that we still have *Midsomer Murders* to give us a true picture of English country life.

Have a go!
Before the war, the BBC would not broadcast anyone with a regional accent, unless it was being used for comic effect. They were persuaded to make an exception during the war by employing Yorkshire actor Wilfred Pickles as a newsreader, on the basis that it would make it more difficult for the Nazis to impersonate BBC broadcasters (imagine Lord Haw Haw trying to do a Yorkshire accent). Once hostilities ceased, Pickles was asked to come up with a programme that engaged with the working man, and he suggested the title *Have a go!* It had its own theme tune, in which the audience joined in (all together now):

> Have a go, Joe, come on and have a go,
> You can't lose out, it costs you nowt
> To make yourself some dough.
> So hurry up and join us,
> Don't be shy and don't be slow
> Come on Joe, have a go!

He was assisted by Violet Carson (later to find fame on *Coronation Street* as Ena Sharples) at the piano, and his wife Mabel at the table dispensing prize money which could make the contestants rich beyond their wildest dreams (provided those dreams did not extend beyond the jackpot prize of £1 19s 11d – that's almost a full £2!). Participants would have to answer questions and relate heart-warming anecdotes to get their hands on the prize money. Not everyone loved the show; critics accused it of sentimentality and Pickles of nauseating cheerfulness. However, the show ran from 1946–67 and, at its peak, commanded listening figures of around 20 million. A television spin-off from the show, *Ask Pickles*, actually beat *I Love Lucy* in the ratings in October 1955.

Educating Archie

Peter Brough was a spectacularly bad ventriloquist – his lips used to move more than the dummy's – so he took the sensible (if improbable) step of building a career as a radio ventriloquist (radio mime artist presumably not being a viable alternative). *Educating Archie* was to run from 1950–58, and was broadly built around the education of the dummy, Archie Andrews, who was portrayed as a smart-Alec teenager. Its cast list reads like a who's who of British comedy. The show's writers included Eric Sykes and Marty Feldman, and the cast list at various times featured Harry Secombe, Tony Hancock, Alfred Marks, Bernard Miles, Gilbert Harding, Bruce Forsyth, Sid James, Max Bygraves and Hattie Jacques. Beryl Reid was on hand to develop her characters Monica (the St Trinians-style schoolgirl) and Brummie Marlene, and a thirteen-year-old Julie Andrews played Archie's girlfriend.

The show was hugely popular, drawing audiences of up to 15 million, and winning the *Daily Mail* National Radio Awards three years running (1951–53). It also made lots of money (or as much money as rationing permitted, at first) through the merchandising of Archie Andrews soap, lollies, comics and other products. Whether any of these were consumed by the Royal Family is not known, but they were apparently avid listeners of the show. On several occasions the dummy went missing, and was even kidnapped once. (How did the kidnappers inform Brough? Common kidnap practice is to send proof of life of the victim through the post – did they perhaps send him some wood shavings? In any event, the dummy eventually turned up in the lost property office at Kings Cross Station.) The show also made the transition to television in 1956. Whilst quite a lot of people obviously found Archie cute, some (including Brough's daughter) found his manic, staring eyes deeply sinister.

The Clitheroe Kid

This followed the adventures of a mischievous eleven-year-old, northern schoolboy, who was constantly getting himself and the other characters into scrapes. Jimmy Clitheroe was in fact aged thirty-five when he took on the part, but had no trouble slotting into it, since he never grew to be more than 4ft 3in tall. He would wear a schoolboy cap and blazer, even for the radio recordings, to add verisimilitude. The radio programme ran from 1957–72, attracting audiences of up to 10 million. Before that, Clitheroe had a long career on stage, including sixteen Blackpool Summer Seasons and two years working with Ken Dodd, and in films, including one with George Formby. The humour in the programme can safely be described as 'schoolboy'.

Mrs Dale's Diary

The London suburb of Parkwood Hill (again, mysteriously absent from my A-Z of London …) was the setting for a soap opera about the lives of a Dr Jim Dale, his wife, Mary, and their family and neighbours. Between 1948 and 1969 it provided the Queen Mother with 'the only way of knowing what goes on in a middle-class family'. The Queen Mother was something of a minority in her listening habits. A 1951 survey showed that only

25 per cent of the upper-middle classes (the nearest category the survey had to royalty) listened to it regularly, whereas 52 per cent of the working class tuned in religiously. Just as *The Archers* became a vehicle for relaying farming hints, so Dr Jim Dale was well-placed to dispense medical advice on any topical illnesses.

In its lifetime, the programme survived a move from Radio 4 to Radio 2, a modernisation (becoming just *The Dales*) and the fictional family's relocation from London to the new town of Exton. It was a quintessentially middle-class programme, and Mrs Dale's repeated lament of 'I'm rather worried about Jim' became the butt of much satire, featuring in *The Goons* (who fantasised about Mrs Dale in her nightshirt being chased by Richard Dimbleby), *The Glums*, *Private Eye* and *Round the Horne* (in whose hands it became *Mrs Dire's Dreary*). Nonetheless, it attracted over 6 million listeners daily. It is also notable for being the first mainstream British drama to feature an overtly homosexual character – Sally's husband, Mrs Dale's brother-in-law – and to treat them sympathetically. This aside, what listeners seemed to like most about the programme (according to the *Radio Times*) was 'Its stable continuity and the absence of any harrowing tragedies.' (Characteristics it had in common with those early television intervals featuring the potter's wheel.)

The Goons

Broadcast from 1951 to 1960 (originally under the title *Crazy People) The Goon Show* is one of the most durable, and certainly the most original, radio outputs of the 1950s. It was mostly written by Spike Milligan, though when the pressure of doing so contributed to his nervous breakdowns, others such as Eric Sykes and John Antrobus took his place and managed to replicate faithfully the Milligan tone. This style has been described as 'ludicrous plots, surreal humour, puns, catch-phrases and an array of bizarre sound effects' and it has influenced British comedy ever since – the Monty Python team, Peter Cook, the Beatles and Eddie Izzard have all acknowledged their debt to *The Goons*. Naturally, BBC executives were hesitant about broadcasting it at all and, having done so, cordially hated it. The show's producer counted at least thirty attempts to have it taken off the air.

The format of the shows, as they evolved, was a three-act narrative separated by musical interludes, in which Harry Secombe played Neddy Seagoon, a likeable but gullible and greedy character, and the nearest thing the show had to either a hero or a straight man. All around him, Milligan and Peter Sellars populated the show with demented characters, the mere naming of whom would, even today, lead to devotees coming out with the silly voices and catchphrases.

Milligan played (among others):

※ Eccles – characterised mainly by his stupidity

※ Minnie Bannister – lusty female senior citizen

※ Count Jim Moriarty – a degraded and impoverished lackey to Grytpype-Thynne

※ Little Jim – a small boy

While Sellars' characters included:

※ Bluebottle – a young boy scout

※ Henry Crun – crumbling old wreck and would-be paramour to Minnie Bannister

※ Major Denis Bloodnok – cowardly ex-army man and crook, with severe digestive problems

※ Hercules Grytpype-Thynne – suave crook and conman

As for catchphrases, who could forget:

※ 'He's fallen in the water!' (Little Jim)

※ 'You dirty rotten swine, you! You've deaded me!' (Bluebottle)

※ 'You can't get the wood, you know' (Henry Crun)

✳ 'You silly, twisted boy, you!' (Grytpype-Thynne)

✳ 'No more curried eggs for me!' (This was preceded by a loud explosion and sounds of a chicken squawking)

✳ 'Nurse! The screens!' (Bloodnok)

And this is for Auntie Edna ...
At the end of the 1950s, the show with the largest radio audience was a testament to remaining delusions of imperial greatness held by the nation. *Two-Way Family Favourites* was a record request programme, in which messages were sent between British families and family members serving as part of the occupying forces in post-war Germany (sometimes it was extended to cover other outposts of Empire). It was broadcast from midday on a Sunday, and a whole generation will be unable to think of the programme without smelling Sunday lunch cooking.

Naughty Boys and Bad Girls

This section contains an assortment of people who, in one way or another, managed to outrage 1950s public opinion. It has to be said that not all of the candidates can be described as equally naughty/bad. They range from mass murderers (one of them suspected, rather than proven), to spies and traitors, to some whose only assaults were on the eyes or ears, and from which the public soon recovered.

The 'can't do it' man: Reginald Christie

Timothy Evans and his wife, Beryl, moved into the top-floor flat of a run-down property at 10 Rillington Place, Notting Hill, during Easter of 1948. In October of that year, Beryl gave birth to their daughter, Geraldine. Late in 1949, Evans reported the death of his wife to the police. The police found the bodies of both Beryl and Geraldine in a wash house at the back of the property – both had been strangled and Beryl had been assaulted prior to her death. Evans initially accused a fellow tenant, Reginald Christie, of the crime, which he said had followed a botched abortion. Evans later 'confessed' to the crime, but his statement was riddled with contradictions, and it is now believed that it was fabricated by the police; the confession was subsequently withdrawn by Evans. He was an easy target for the prosecution – it was an unhappy and occasionally violent marriage, he was illiterate and had an IQ of about 70 and did not make a persuasive witness. Christie featured as a main prosecution witness in the Evans case, which resulted in his conviction for the murders. Evans was hanged in March 1950.

Details of Christie's criminal record (involving thefts and at least one case of violence towards a woman) emerged at the trial, but apparently did not affect his credibility as a witness. Nor had it troubled the police in 1939, when they recruited Christie as a War Reserve Police Officer, apparently without checking his background. The police also missed other clues in the course of their investigation, such as the human thigh bone that was being used to prop up the fence, and it was years before the full extent of the horrors of 10 Rillington Place emerged.

It was in March 1953, just after Christie had moved out, that prospective tenants (who were already wondering about the funny smell in the flat) discovered a hidden coal store containing the remains of three women. The police were called and their forensic skills immediately told them that something was amiss. Further investigation revealed the former Mrs Ethel Christie beneath some loose floorboards. Christie was tracked down and asked to explain, and his account fell some way short of convincing.

Ethel, he said, had been suffering from depression due to a dispute with fellow tenants and had been taking barbiturates. One evening, he had found her dying from an overdose and had struggled, without success, to revive her (which sat uneasily with the absence of barbiturates in her body and the marks of her strangulation). He claimed that he left her in bed for a couple of days, then buried her beneath the floorboards because he could not bear to be parted from her (a form of husbandly devotion most of the jury had not previously encountered). At the same time, he had given all sorts of excuses for her absence to her friends – that she could not write due to rheumatism, or that she had gone on extended visits to Birmingham or Sheffield.

However, this did not account for the other bodies inconveniently lying around the flat. Christie's defence of 'I just blacked out and when I came round, there she was strangled' in relation to one of his victims did not cut much ice with the judge. It emerged that the victims were, for the most part, prostitutes which he lured back to his flat (in one case with the promise of a cure for catarrh), where he had gassed them and sexually assaulted them as they lay dying, then strangled them to finish them off. Christie had a history of sexual impotence – he had been nicknamed 'Reggie-no-Dick' and 'Can't-do-it Christie' in his youth, and could normally only perform with prostitutes.

He was only charged with the murder of his wife, but was thought to have been responsible for at least eight murders between 1943 and 1953. He was hanged at Pentonville Prison in July 1953. As his arms were being strapped up for execution, he apparently complained to the hangman that his nose was itching. Executioner Mr Pierrepoint replied, 'Don't worry; it won't trouble you for long.'

Timothy Evans was pardoned in October 1966 for the crimes of which he had been convicted (and, more to the point, hanged). Rillington Place was renamed Ruston Close in response to a petition from the residents, and was eventually demolished.

One who got away?
Doctor John Bodkin Adams

Harold Shipman is the only General Practitioner ever to be found guilty of the mass murder of his patients, but there was a case in the 1950s that many thought was equally horrifying, if not worse. John Bodkin Adams was born in Antrim in 1899, the son of a Plymouth Brethren lay preacher. He studied medicine, showing little promise as a student, but graduated and moved to Eastbourne in 1922. Then, as now, it was a town where wealthy elderly ladies were more numerous than the stones on the beach, and Adams' comforting bedside manner compensated for any shortcomings in his technical competence. Over the next thirty-five years, he became possibly the richest GP in the country.

His practice was characterised by two features. One was his willingness to help his patients alter their wills, with himself as a beneficiary, coupled with a request to be cremated. The other was the wildly excessive doses of painkillers that he prescribed them. Two cases in the 1950s (first revealed in print in *Paris Match*, safely out of the reach of the British libel laws) drew him to the attention of the police. One was that of Edith Morell, who had been partly paralysed after a stroke. The other was Gertrude Hullett, a mere child (by Eastbourne standards) at fifty, who was depressed to the point of suicide after the death of her husband, and who eventually died of barbiturate poisoning. Both women left Adams gifts, including Rolls-Royce cars, in their wills. Police investigators came up with no less than 163 'suspicious' deaths associated with Adams, but he was put on trial in relation to just a specimen charge – the death of Mrs Morrell – in March 1957.

The press loved this sensational case and the blood-curdling headlines it gave them. One American publication managed to link Adams with some 400 deaths. The defence managed to pull one rabbit out of the hat, in the form of a detailed record of all the medication given to Mrs Morrell by Dr Adams, which had been overlooked by the prosecution, but most people still assumed he was guilty. It was a sensation when the jury took just forty-five minutes to acquit him.

Conspiracy theorists had a field day. Adams was known to have powerful friends in the political world and one suggestion was that the Attorney General might have intervened in some way, driven by the fact that a guilty verdict might have sparked a revolt amongst the medical profession in the fledgling National Health Service. A further consideration was that Adams had made dark, if non-specific, threats about 'naming names' should he be found guilty and have to go to appeal. The Government was already unpopular after the Suez debacle, and might not have survived another major scandal.

Others were out-and-out supporters of Adams, arguing that he was a mercy killer, protecting his patients from undue suffering during their terminal illnesses at a time when there was little palliative medicine available to the medical profession. As for his patients' 'bequests', his apologists would argue that they were relatively small in relation to the patients' overall wealth. They would also point out that it was a not uncommon (if gruesome) practice for doctors in those days to give their private patients much reduced bills during their lifetime, on the understanding that they would be 'remembered' in their wills. Finally, the point was made that Adams had kept Mrs Morrell alive far longer than the life expectancy of one year that she had been given after her stroke.

After the trial, Adams resigned from the National Health Service and sold his story to the *Daily Express* (one of the few papers not to have condemned him in advance) for £10,000. He was later struck off for forging prescriptions, but reinstated as a GP in 1961. When he died, a free man, in 1983, he was worth £402,970.

'Let him have it!'
Derek Bentley and Christopher Craig

Derek Bentley did not have the easiest start in life. A fall on his head during childhood caused him to develop epilepsy and he was traumatised by being repeatedly bombed out of his home during the Second World War. Later tests showed him to have an IQ of 77, making him (in the politically incorrect terminology of the day) 'borderline feeble-minded'. He was judged to have a mental age of eleven and could neither read nor write. Unsurprisingly, he was turned down for military service, sacked from various jobs and got in trouble with the law.

By the age of nineteen, he had fallen under the influence of a sixteen-year-old tearaway called Christopher Craig, and they hatched a plot to break into a warehouse in Croydon. Bentley took with him a spiked knuckleduster and a knife, but Craig was armed with a sawn-off service revolver from the First World War. They were seen climbing the warehouse fence, the police were called and they were cornered on the warehouse roof. One of the officers, a Detective Sergeant Fairfax, managed to grab Bentley, despite being slightly wounded by a gunshot – Bentley did not try to use his weapons on the officer.

At this point, police officers claim that Bentley shouted to Craig, 'Let him have it, Chris!', but this is something that both Craig and Bentley consistently denied. Another officer, PC Sidney Miles, was then shot fatally in the head. When he ran out of ammunition, Craig tried to escape by jumping 30ft off the warehouse roof into a greenhouse, breaking his back and wrist.

At the subsequent trial, a number of issues came up. First, how many shots were fired and by whom? The fatal bullet was never found. The police had also been armed, and one of the spent bullets found at the crime scene was of their calibre. The picture was further confused by Craig's gun having been modified to fire different calibres of bullet. Second, were the words 'Let him have it, Chris!' ever said and, if so, what did they mean? They were clearly capable of more than one interpretation – did it mean 'Shoot!' or 'I say, Christopher, be a frightfully good chap and surrender your firearm to the officer'?

The third issue was Bentley's fitness to stand trial. At this time, English law did not recognise the principle of diminished responsibility and Bentley did not pass the test of full-blown criminal insanity. The law of the day also stated that an unpremeditated death caused during the commission of a felony counted as murder – what they called the principle of constructive malice. Although nobody suggested that Bentley actually fired the fatal shot, their joint decision to commit the break-in (and his controversial alleged incitement to Craig to use the gun) made Bentley and Craig equally culpable in the eyes of the law of the 1950s.

In fact, Bentley had more to lose. Craig fell below the minimum age for the death penalty, but Bentley was over eighteen and, therefore, could be hanged. So, while Craig was detained at Her Majesty's pleasure (he was released in May 1963, after ten years), Bentley received the death penalty. Despite campaigns for leniency – starting with a plea for clemency for Bentley from the jury, and including a petition signed by 200 Members of Parliament, another with 12,000 signatures collected by Bentley's family and demonstrations outside the prison – the Home Secretary decided in January 1953 that the death penalty would go ahead. Hours before the execution, Labour MP, R.T. Paget spoke angrily of the case, after the Speaker refused to allow a debate on the Home Secretary's decision: 'A three-quarter-witted boy of nineteen is to be hanged for a murder which he did not commit and which was committed fifteen minutes after he was arrested.'

This marked the start of a long campaign for justice, resulting in changes to the law (the Homicide Act of 1957), a Royal Pardon for Bentley in 1993 and the quashing of the conviction itself in 1998. The Lord Chief Justice's quashing of the conviction produced a very critical assessment of the trial judge's 'blatantly prejudiced' summing up, and of the pressure asserted on the jurors to convict. (During the course of trial, he had theatrically produced Bentley's knuckleduster as a prop.) There had also subsequently been some suggestion that the police were 'selective' in the evidence they put before the court.

Hell hath no fury ... Ruth Ellis

Ruth Ellis suffered violent abuse from men all her life – first from her father, then from her drunken ex-husband and finally from her playboy racing-driver boyfriend, David Blakely. She would regularly appear in public bruised and battered and, ten days before the key event took place, Blakely was said to have punched her in the stomach, causing her to miscarry their child.

She appeared before the court in June 1955. The central facts of her case were simple and undisputed. She was a twenty-eight-year-old, euphemistically described as a nightclub hostess or model, who had been in a volatile relationship with Blakely. He had been consorting with other women and wanted to end things with Ellis, and left her at Easter to stay with friends at Hampstead. She followed him and shot him four times with a revolver as he came out of a pub, before trying to shoot herself, but the gun jammed and instead she handed herself in to an off-duty policeman who had been having a drink in the pub. So far, so clear.

The verdict was never in doubt once the trial judge, Sir Cecil Havers, refused to allow Ellis' counsel to argue provocation as a defence. The jury took twenty-three minutes to find her guilty of the killing, and the judge had no choice but to order the death sentence as outlined by law. The central issue at her trial had related to what the French call the *crime passionnel*. Had the balance of her mind been so upset that she could be found guilty of the lesser crime of manslaughter? Ellis did not appeal against the verdict, but entered a plea for clemency with the Home Secretary. He was unmoved by the petitions and demonstrations that followed, and, on 13 July 1955, Ruth Ellis was hanged at Holloway Prison, becoming the last woman to be executed in Britain.

The French were particularly struck by this case. At about the same time, they were dealing with a very similar case in which a Corsican woman had been found guilty of a murder and had received a two-year suspended sentence. The French were puzzled that English law made no distinction between the cold-blooded killer, the opportunist who murdered in the commission of a crime, and the perpetrator of a crime of passion, who was unlikely to re-offend. Nor did there appear to be much consistency in the way murderers' appeals for clemency were handled. In the week of Ellis' execution, another woman in Britain was granted a reprieve, having battered her eighty-six-year-old neighbour to death with a shovel in the course of a feud. The American crime writer Raymond Chandler wrote in the *Evening Standard* on 30 June,

'This was a crime of passion under considerable provocation. No other country in the world would hang this woman.'

As we have seen, the law prior to 1957 did not recognise the idea of diminished responsibility, and a defence of provocation required it to be an immediate reaction in the heat of the moment – Ellis' action was held to be more premeditated. The Home Secretary thought that much of the fuss relating to her case stemmed from the fact that she was an attractive woman, and was not prepared to apply different standards to the sexes. But the argument probably cut both ways – along with the sympathy many felt for the (normally) gentler sex, part of public opinion (particularly female) probably looked at her peroxide blonde hair and pencilled eyebrows and concluded that she was 'no better than she ought to be'. The Home Secretary also thought that a reprieve in Ellis' case would call into question the very existence of the death penalty. He was correct in his assumption, because Ellis' case was to be an important argument in the 1965 debate about its abolition. As Frederick Raphael put it: 'I daresay she was a vulgar little tart with a predilection for wearing crosses round her neck, but to sentence her to die at such and such a time, in that way is to make her into a dying goddess.'

I-spy: 1
Klaus Fuchs

In 1933, a young student physicist fled to England from Germany. He was a Quaker and a leading agitator for the German Communist Party, and it was clear that his prospects in Nazi Germany would be exceedingly bleak. Klaus Fuchs enrolled at Bristol University, and he was awarded a PhD in 1937. Along with most German nationals in Britain during the war, he was interned, but it did not take the authorities long to recognise his potential value to the war effort and he was released in December 1940, to work on the 'Tube Alloys Programme', which was actually the development of a British atomic bomb. British citizenship followed in 1942, and the following year he became part of the British team that went to America to contribute to the Manhattan Project, which would lead to Hiroshima.

Fuchs was hiding a dark secret. From as early as August 1941, he had been in contact with the Russian spy network, passing secrets to them. It is thought his motivation may have been a realisation of the awesome power of his project, and that felt that it should not be left in the hands of a single nation. By sharing it with the Russians, he hoped to achieve deterrence. Thus, Russia had the instructions for making a bomb, months before the end of the war with Japan. He also briefed them on America's state of readiness for nuclear war in the late 1940s to early 1950s.

When he returned home, he was made head of the Theoretical Physics Division at the Atomic Weapons Research Establishment at Harwell. By this time, a defecting KGB officer had alerted the British authorities to the existence of a Communist spy ring among them. Fuchs was one of those interrogated during the rounding up of the agents, but his cover remained intact until January 1950, when he readily confessed to giving secrets to the Russians, although he would not tell the MI5 officer what he had handed over, since the officer interrogating him was apparently not cleared for such a high level of secret. It seems Fuchs naively failed to appreciate the gravity of what he had done, and thought he could return to his work at Harwell, once the matter had been cleared up. Instead, he was swiftly brought to trial and sentenced

to fourteen years in prison – the maximum possible sentence for a breach of the Official Secrets Act. The trial was kept as low-key as possible, not least because the British authorities did not want details of their atomic bomb programme going public.

Upon his release from prison in June 1959, Fuchs emigrated to East Germany, where he was given senior appointments in their scientific community and showered with honours. He died there in 1988. It remains unclear how important Fuchs' betrayal was; handing over the recipe for an atomic bomb sounds about as serious as it gets, but how much did the Russians already know, and how much would they have been able to work out for themselves? It was also known that the head of Russian espionage, Lavrenti Beria, distrusted scientific intelligence and used it to double-check other sources, rather than handing it over to scientists who might have been better able to use it. One definite consequence of his activities was a loss of confidence that scuppered plans for Britain to receive supplies of American-made atomic bombs.

I spy: 2
The Cambridge spies - and a crabb!

Pre-war Cambridge University was a fertile recruiting ground for Russian espionage. In particular, there was an exclusive and secretive debating society called the Apostles, from which came four of the most important Russian spies – Donald Maclean, Guy Burgess, Harold 'Kim' Philby and Anthony Blunt. A fifth man – often named as John Cairncross – was also known to be working for the Russians. Philby and Burgess even went as far as joining the pro-Nazi Anglo-German Fellowship in 1934, as a means of hiding their true leanings.

After university, Burgess started out as a radio producer, but joined MI6 as an intelligence officer at the outbreak of war. Philby, in an inspired appointment during the later war years, was made head of MI6's anti-Soviet section, and later chief of British intelligence in America. Maclean, son of Liberal MP and one-time Leader of the Opposition, Sir Donald Maclean, went to work at the Foreign Office, being posted, *inter alia*, to Paris and Washington. Blunt, third cousin to the Queen Mother, joined MI5 during the war and later went on to be a distinguished art historian (for twenty-seven years he was Surveyor of the King's [and later the Queen's] Pictures). Between them, they passed on decodes of Enigma transmissions from Bletchley Park, reports on the British atomic bomb project and details of discussions between the British and American governments, first about the conduct of the war and later about countering the Soviet Cold War menace.

By 1951, Philby learned that Maclean was on the verge of being exposed as a spy. He arranged for Burgess (then based in Washington, where he was proving to be something of an embarrassment with his drinking and his predatory homosexuality) to be returned to London, where he could tip off Maclean. The MI5 began arrangements to question Maclean on 28 May 1951. On the preceding Friday, Burgess and Maclean vanished, not to be seen again for five years.

In February 1956, two weeks after Soviet leader Nikita Kruschchev denied their presence in the USSR, Burgess and Maclean surfaced at a Moscow press conference, where they improbably denied any involvement in espionage. Their exposure as spies inevitably threw suspicion on the others. Philby was forced to resign from MI6, although he was not charged with any offence. He was named as a spy in the press, but the then Foreign Secretary, Harold Macmillan, completely exonerated him due to incomplete information and shoddy investigation by British intelligence. Philby later went to work as a journalist in the Middle East, where his reporting was said to be a cover for further work for MI6 (and the KGB?). He finally defected to Russia in 1963. Blunt was known (or suspected) to be a spy for many years. He confessed to it in 1963, in return for a promise of immunity if he revealed all he knew about Soviet espionage activity in Britain. Only in 1979 did his treachery become public knowledge. As with the Fuchs case, the Government deliberately kept it low-key, partly for fear of sparking off a McCarthy-style witch-hunt. As Harold Macmillan put it, 'Nothing could be worse than a lot of muck-raking and innuendo. It would be like one of those immense divorce cases which they used to have when I was young, going on for days and days, every detail reported in the press.'

The failure of British intelligence to uncover traitors in their ranks quickly seemed, in part, to be a result of their inability to believe that 'one of us' could do anything so unsporting. Among the effects of this espionage is the serious damage done to the Anglo-American 'special relationship' in the 1950s.

Of course, spying for the other side is a thoroughly disreputable business, but spying for us is an entirely different matter. Another big espionage scandal of the 1950s concerned one of our spies – Lionel 'Buster' Crabb. Crabb was a Royal Navy diver, and something of a war hero. In April 1956, Nikita Kruschchev arrived in Britain on board a Soviet cruiser. Crabb was sent to look at the ship's underside, to find out about a new type of propeller – not the first time he had been sent on such a mission. He jumped into Portsmouth Harbour – and promptly disappeared. Fourteen months later, a headless, handless (and, therefore, in those days, conveniently unidentifiable) corpse washed up in a frogman's suit. The assumption was made that the body was Crabb.

There were many theories about his disappearance. The Royal Navy's cover story was that he died testing new diving equipment. The press said he had been kidnapped by the Russians and taken to Moscow. One Russian account had him being killed by one of their own frogmen whilst trying to place a mine on the cruiser, and another had him shot by a Soviet sniper. There were even conspiracy theorists who said MI5 had killed him, to stop him defecting to the Russians. The official papers relating to the case are not due to be released until 2057 – and even then, the full truth may not emerge.

Wanted for offences against taste

Lady Norma Docker

'We bring glamour and happiness into otherwise drab lives. The working classes love everything we do.'

(Lady Docker)

It would be unfair to classify our final examples as bad girls and boys, as they are not quite in the same league as murderers, spies and other serious miscreants – unless you were a shareholder in Daimler, a lover of rare species or a spokesperson for good taste. Norma Royce Turner was born above a butcher's shop in Derby in 1906. After her father committed suicide when she was only sixteen, Norma Docker supported herself by becoming a dance hostess at the Café de Paris in London. She was soon able to charge her partners the premium rate of £1 per dance, and got to meet some very wealthy and influential men, three of whom she married in short order. First, there was Clement Callingham, head of a wine and spirit company, who died in 1945. The following year she married Sir William Collins, who was (among other things) the president of luxury grocers Fortnum & Mason. He was sixty-nine when they married, and he only lasted until 1948.

However, her real claim to fame began with her third marriage, in 1949, to Sir Bernard Docker, chairman of Daimler and its parent company BSA, and a director of the travel company, Thomas Cook. Married at last to one of the richest men in Britain, Lady Docker (as she was now titled) could indulge her outrageous taste and hedonism, apparently without boundaries. Sir Bernard already had a large yacht, so some of Lady Docker's most high-profile indulgences were a series of spectacularly customised Daimler limousines. On these, anything that would normally be chromium was gold-plated and the interior fittings on them read like a list of exhibits at London Zoo, featuring a variety of upholstery from lizard skin, alligator or zebra skin. The zebra-skinned car also boasted an ivory dashboard. Asked why she chose zebra skin, Lady Docker famously replied, 'Because mink is too hot to sit on'.

In addition to her consumer choices, Lady Docker was adept at upsetting people. She fell out with Prince Rainier of Monaco to such an extent that he barred her from the Principality (typically, she responded by threatening to build a casino to rival Monte Carlo). When news of this ban reached Essex, the authorities at Canvey Island invited her to come and open their carnival, a task that she undertook with great enthusiasm. She also told councillors at Morecombe, who had upset her, to go and jump in the bay, and was taken to court for assaulting an Italian police officer in Capri.

The publicity surrounding their lavish lifestyle – not to mention some extremely questionable accounting practices in writing off his outgoings as business expenses – eventually grew too much for Sir Bernard's employers and, in the mid-1950s, he was dismissed from his various directorships. Daimler took back all the customised limousines, and Norma responded by ordering a Bentley Continental from their rivals. However, this marked a downturn in their fortunes. By 1965, Sir Bernard was forced to sell his 860-ton yacht, the *Shemara*, for less than half its £600,000 asking price and, by 1966, their Hampshire estate was sold and they were reduced to living in a tiny bungalow in Jersey, as tax exiles. Characteristically, Norma endeared herself to her new neighbours by publicly saying that the people of Jersey were 'the most frightfully boring, dreadful people that have ever been born'.

In some areas, her vulgar ostentation during a time of austerity attracted public hostility, and 'a Lady Docker' became a term of abuse in some parts of northern England, meaning someone who has pretentions above their station. In other areas, it endeared her to the population and, as she rightly recognised, her outrageous behaviour brought colour into their straitened lives, and, most importantly, she had the common touch. To put it another way, she was as common as muck, with the names 'Lady Docker' and 'Lady Muck' interchangeable in some quarters. She smoked a clay pipe and once invited forty-five miners to a champagne party on board their yacht. She was a keen conkers and marbles player, playing for the BSA Ladies' marbles team, where she sometimes cheated; Docker had her own gold satin cushion to kneel on whilst playing, and a personal marbles coach.

Lady Docker died in 1983 and is buried in a churchyard near Maidenhead – no doubt in a zebra-skin lined coffin.

Wladziu Valentino Liberace

He was a man who had pure syrup running through his veins, who played piano with prodigious virtuosity and execrable taste, and who dressed in a manner that made Lady Docker look positively dowdy. Liberace (Lee to his friends, Walter to his family) was born in Wisconsin in 1919, to a Polish mother and an Italian father. He started playing the piano at the age of four and soon demonstrated a considerable aptitude for it, memorising complex pieces by the age of seven. He was an admirer (and later family friend) of the great Polish virtuoso Paderewski and, at the age of twenty-one, performed Liszt's *Second Piano Concerto* with the Chicago Symphony Orchestra. He also performed for President Truman at the White House.

However, other forces led him away from a conventional classical career. He began to develop a repertoire that combined popular tunes with easy listening versions of the classics and banter and jokes with his audience. At the same time, he started to wear ever more elaborate and bizarre costumes, and to have the most lavish possible staging for his performances. He also took to singing – in particular, his theme-tune, *I'll Be Seeing You*. Those who liked that sort of thing loved him, and during the 1950s and 1960s he became the highest-paid entertainer in the world. He needed to be, as his spending habits threatened to outstrip even his lavish income. He bought show-houses with piano-shaped swimming pools, stuffed with priceless antiques.

On stage, his predilection for dressing up and showing off got out of control. He would have five or six costume changes per show – and what costumes! They included:

* A Norwegian blue shadow fox fur cape that had a 16ft by 12ft train. He boasted to his audience that there were only two of them in the world, and that he owned them both. (The real surprise was that there were two of them)

* A pink, glass suit embroidered with silver beads, which literally lit up as he played

* A cape costing $60,000 that threatened the very survival of chinchillas as a species

* A tuxedo with his name embroidered in diamonds across it

* A King Neptune costume, inlaid with pearls and shells, and weighing 200lb

The only time he was ever more understated than the person he was with was when he met the Pope – for which he wore a plain business suit. To add to the visual impact of his shows, he would be lowered onto the stage by wires, or chauffeured on in a Rolls-Royce. In addition to his purely (if that is the word) musical performances, he appeared as a guest on the

Muppet Show (where even Miss Piggy would have struggled to out-dress him) and in the highly camp 1960s television version of *Batman*.

Mainstream music critics hated him. Here is the verdict of one Louis Funke: 'Liberace recreates – if that is the word – each composition in his own image, "When it is too difficult, he simplifies it. When it is too simple, he complicates it."'

He accused Liberace of 'slackness of rhythms, wrong tempos, distorted phrasing, an excess of prettification and sentimentality and a failure to stick to what the composer has written.'

His dress code alone might have led people to question his sexuality, and, in 1956, the *Daily Mirror* columnist Cassandra went too far in a not-entirely favourable review that described him as:

> The summit of sex – the pinnacle of masculine, feminine and neuter. Everything that he, she and it can ever want … a deadly, winking, sniggering, chromium-plated, scent-impregnated, luminous, quivering, giggling, fruit-flavoured, mincing, ice-covered heap of mother love … The biggest vomit of all time.

Liberace's lawyers claimed that this splendid heap of invective implied that their client was homosexual (at that time illegal, and certainly something that would have affected his standing with the middle-aged ladies) and he won £8,000 in damages. Asked later how much this accusation had hurt him, he famously replied that he had cried all the way to the bank. However, suggestions of homosexuality continued to haunt him, in particular when he fired Scott Thorson, his twenty-four-year-old chauffeur, who then went public with claims that he had really been Liberace's live-in lover. He was forced to make a generous out-of-court settlement with his former employee.

Liberace opened a museum to himself in Las Vegas, his spiritual home, in 1978. In 1987, he died from pneumonia resulting from AIDS. In his favour, it must be said that he did not take himself entirely seriously (were such a thing possible). He would flaunt his diamond rings to his audience and ask, 'Do you like them? You should do – you paid for them', and referred to himself as 'a one-man Disneyland'. He also left a positive legacy in the Liberace Foundation, a charity that helps talented students pursue careers in the performing arts.

Sporting Disasters

We hear enough about sporting triumphs, so let's look instead at some of the sporting disasters – of varying degrees of disastrousness – that befell Britain or the British over the decade.

Humbled by foreigners

USA 1 England 0

England missed the first three World Cups, due to a row with the organising body over payments to amateur players, but by 1950 the dispute was resolved and the England team travelled to Brazil as 3/1 favourites to win the cup. England were at that time regarded (not least by themselves) as the world's number one side, with a post-war record of twenty-three wins, three draws and only four defeats. They had beaten Portugal 10–0 just two weeks before. The first World Cup game – a 2–0 victory over Chile – went according to the script, and for their second match they faced the part-timers of the United States.

Nobody gave the USA a hope – they had only trained together once before the match and had lost their last seven matches by an aggregate score of 45–2. The *Daily Express* even suggested that it would be only fair to give them a three-goal start. England's star turn, Stanley Matthews, had joined the squad late and was rested from this match, to keep him fresh for the more serious opposition. No matter – the rest of the heavyweight England team would be more than enough to bulldoze the opposition … or so they thought.

There is no doubt that England dominated the play, however, they did everything but score. Then, in the 37th minute, a diving header by the United States' Joe Gaetjens left England goalkeeper Bert Williams stranded. At half time, the unimaginable score-line was USA 1 England 0. England created more chances in the second half, with a similar lack of success, but so did the USA. At one point, England defender (and future manager) Alf Ramsey had to perform a sliding clearance off the line, as an American shot headed for an empty net. The match ended 1–0. England went on to lose their final pool match (1–0 to Spain) and so made an early exit from the very competition that they were expected to win.

The result had little immediate impact at home. Post-war austerity, and the shortage of newsprint that went with it, meant that papers could only devote one page to sports coverage. That same day, another England defeat – by the West Indies at cricket – took centre stage. There were even reports (later denied) that the result had been so unexpected that press reporters had misread it as a 10–0 win to England.

There were later claims that the USA team had been an 'Ellis Island XI' illegally consisting of foreign immigrants, but an investigation by FIFA found that eight of the team were USA-born, while the other three qualified under the regulations to play for them. England's footballing invincibility had suffered its first dent – it would not be the last.

England 3 Hungary 6

'If it wasn't for the English you'd be Krauts' sang the satirical home fans as the two sides turned out at Wembley for the

England v Hungary football match in November 1953. Despite earlier experience at the hands of the United States 'no-hopers', most of England's assessment of foreigners playing football was like Dr Johnson's view of women preaching, or dogs walking on their hind legs – you did not expect to see it done well, but you are surprised to see it done at all. However, if the Hungarian fans understood a word of what our lot were singing about, they would be entitled by the end of the game to respond with a chorus of 'You're not singing anymore', or whatever that is in Hungarian.

No matter that the Hungarians were then ranked world number one team and were Olympic champions, undefeated in twenty-four games. Their star player, Puskas (unknown in Britain) was a major in the army – not even a full-time professional! Besides, we had Stanley Matthews, fresh from his Wembley triumph – *and* we invented the game! (This caused the press to bill it as 'the match of the century' and it drew a crowd of 105,000.) Even the Hungarians' kit came in for ridicule, as the England captain Billy Wright recalled:

> When we walked out at Wembley that afternoon, side by side with the visiting team, I looked down and noticed that the Hungarians had on these strange lightweight boots, cut away like slippers under the ankle bone. I turned to big Stan Mortensen and said 'We should be all right here Stan, they haven't got the proper kit'.

England's tactical and physical superiority were taken as given in those days, but for no good reason. As we saw, they only entered the World Cup for the first time in 1950 and the FA would oppose any British club team taking part in the European Cup. The England manager, Walter Winterbottom, had no previous football management experience and team selection was done in a rather haphazard way by an FA committee. The team's starting line-up (known as WM or, in modern parlance, 3.2.2.3) had been devised by Arsenal to overcome a change in the offside rule as long ago as 1925 (but had been designed around the particular strengths of the 1925 Arsenal squad).

The game started badly, with Hungary scoring in the first minute, and went steadily downhill from there. By half time, England was 4–2 behind. Much of the second half was a demonstration in Hungarian possession play; Hungary had thirty-five shots on target and eventually ran out 6–3 winners.

England had only ever suffered one home defeat to foreigners before this (to the Republic of Ireland in 1949 – which hardly counted, since they had only recently stopped being British). The result traumatised English football. Six of the England team that day never played for their country again, and the best club managers realised that they must learn from the continental way of doing things. Matt Busby defied the FA by entering Manchester United for the European Cup and many of the most successful managers of the next decade or two – Don Revie, Bill Nicholson, Ron Greenwood, Malcolm Allison and Brian Clough – adopted Hungarian coaching methods.

Stung by this freak result, England made the return visit to Budapest the following May to put these upstarts in their place. This time they lost 7–1 – still their worst ever defeat.

Le Mans 1955

This tragedy happened abroad, but with some British involvement. Since it was first run in 1923, the Le Mans twenty-four hour sports car race has been one of the highlights of the sporting calendar, but the race of 1955 would be remembered for all the wrong reasons.

One of the main rivalries in this race was to be between Jaguar and Mercedes Benz. The latter were running their lightweight 300SLR model, whose bodywork was made of a new magnesium alloy called Elektron. However, unlike the Jaguar cars, they were not fitted with the latest disc brakes, but with the less efficient drum variety, which some thought was a contributory cause of the accident. On lap 35, Mike Hawthorn's Jaguar was being closely pursued by veteran French driver, Pierre Levegh, in a

Mercedes. As they entered the pit straight, Hawthorn overtook a much slower Austin Healey 100, driven by Lance Macklin. As he did so, Hawthorn noticed a pit signal telling him to come in for fuel. He immediately applied the brakes, causing Macklin to pull out to avoid him. Levegh could not brake in time to avoid the Healey and, as they collided at 150mph, his car took off, hit an earthen bank and somersaulted into the crowd.

The bonnet separated from the car and scythed through the spectators like a guillotine, decapitating a number of them. Other parts also broke off, each one leaving an 85m stream of carnage. Levegh was thrown from the car (they had no seatbelts) and died instantly of head injuries. The fuel tank ruptured and a fierce fire broke out, hot enough to cause the magnesium alloy of the bodywork to ignite. Frantic rescue workers turned their hoses on the blaze, which actually made the magnesium fire worse – it would be several hours before the blaze was finally extinguished. In addition to Levegh, eighty-three spectators were killed and another 120 injured in what was motor racing's worst ever disaster.

The race organisers were faced with a dilemma. The obvious course of action was to stop the race, but to do so would lead to a rush for the exits and block the access for ambulances. They therefore let it continue, and it was a few hours before some of the spectators elsewhere on the circuit knew anything about the disaster. The Mercedes team, on instruction from their headquarters, withdrew their cars before the end of the race. Jaguar declined to do likewise and went on to win. However, they were treated with contempt by the French press, and Jaguar decided to make no public relations use of the victory.

There was a good deal of debate about whether anyone was responsible, and who that might be. The official inquiry decided that it was a racing accident and that nobody was to blame. In his autobiography, Mike Hawthorn seemed to imply that Macklin was at fault, and Macklin had a libel action pending against him when Hawthorn met his untimely death in a road accident. Others sought to attach the blame to Hawthorn himself, as the one who caused Macklin to swerve, while Mercedes Benz were accused of making the disaster worse, through their use of untried technology (such as the inflammable alloy bodywork). One guilty verdict was delivered against the circuit itself; its safety standards had not been reviewed since the race was first staged (during which time the top speeds of the cars taking part had risen from about 60–185mph). Motor-sports were banned in several countries, pending a review of safety at their circuits. Mercedes Benz withdrew from motor-sport entirely at the end of the season and did not return to it until 1987.

For his part, Lance Macklin walked away from his damaged Healey. The car was later repaired and was sold, in 2011, for £843,000.

Grand Nationals 1951 and 1956

The Grand National is one horse race in which a certain amount of attrition is expected but, even by its standards, the 1951 running of the race was exceptional. It started as a shambles and went steadily downhill from there. The starter set them off prematurely, before half of the thirty-six runners were ready and, in the scramble to get back into contention, seven of them fell at the first fence. A dozen were down before the race had gone half a mile. For a time, strong favourite Arctic Gold was out in front, until he joined the other rider-less horses around him in disposing of his jockey. After the first circuit, only five runners (with an average starting price of 45/1) were still on their feet. Only three horses would eventually finish, and the third finisher only did so after the jockey had been thrown off and remounted. It was won by 40/1 outsider, Nickel Coin.

The 1956 race was famous mainly for the horse that did not win. The Queen Mother's horse, Devon Loch, was strongly fancied and, as the race reached its final stages, those who had backed it were already mentally counting their winnings. On the run in after the last fence, Devon Loch enjoyed a comfortable five-length lead over his nearest rival. Then, just 40 yards from the winning post, the horse appeared to try to jump an invisible fence and landed on its stomach. By the time it struggled back onto its feet, other horses, led by ESB, had passed him.

Many theories have been advanced for this extraordinary turn of events. Initial thoughts that the horse had suffered a heart attack were dismissed, given the speed of his recovery (he lived until 1963). His jockey, Dick Francis (later to become a successful thriller writer) thought that he was spooked by the cheering of the crowd around the winning post, while others put it down to cramp in the hindquarters. It was also suggested that he had slipped on a damp patch on the course, or that the shadow thrown by the water jump fooled him into thinking that it was an additional fence. (There is apparently a precedent for this last theory. In the 1901 running of the National, a horse named Grundon tried to jump a footpath, thinking that it was a fence.)

A pushover: The 1959 United States Grand Prix

This event only qualifies as a disaster if your name happens to be Stirling Moss or Tony Brooks, but it is weird enough to merit a reference. The 1959 United States Grand Prix at Sebring, Florida, was the last race of the championship season, and three drivers were still in with a chance of the World Driver's Championship – Jack Brabham and Stirling Moss in their innovative rear-engined Cooper Climaxes, and Ferrari driver Tony Brooks. The outcome depended not just on how each driver did individually, but also on where his rivals were placed.

The race did not start well for Brooks, who was rammed off the track by his teammate, von Trips, at the first corner. After a precautionary pit stop he was able to continue, but was well down the field. Then Stirling Moss, having led the race, ground to a halt due to broken transmission. By the final lap, Brabham had what looked to be an unassailable lead, when his car started to misfire and then gave up the ghost entirely. He had run out of petrol, having ignored his team manager's advice to put more fuel in, in the interests of lightening his car. He ground to a complete halt about 500 yards from the chequered flag; Brabham began to fear that Brooks could yet overtake him and snatch the championship, so he leapt from the car and began pushing it – uphill – towards the finish.

Crowds at the finish began to look out anxiously for Brabham, as his erstwhile pursuers crossed the line ahead of him. Then he was seen in the distance, advancing to the finish with agonising slowness. Police on motorcycles went to escort him and to keep back the crowds of enthusiastic spectators who wanted to help him push (but who would thereby have ensured his disqualification). After five minutes pushing, Brabham crossed the line and collapsed, exhausted. As Brabham himself later commented, it must have been the first time a racing driver completed a Grand Prix with a motorcycle escort. In the event, Brooks did pass him, but could only finish third, giving the championship to Brabham by four points.

Munich
3 February 1958

When they won the Football League Championship in 1955/56, the Busby Babes of Manchester United had an average age of just twenty-two. They looked set to dominate British football for the next decade. Just days after a particularly superlative display, in which they beat Arsenal 5–4 at Highbury, Manchester United had to play the second leg of a European Cup game, away to Red Star Belgrade. They secured a 3–3 draw, which was enough to get them into the semi-final. On the way back, their plane landed to refuel at Munich in the middle of a snowstorm. Twice the refuelled plane tried to take off. On the third attempt, the plane ran off the runway, hit some buildings and caught fire. The surviving pilot feared the aircraft was going to explode and tried to move survivors away, but goalkeeper Harry Gregg chose to stay and put his life at risk helping others out of the plane.

According to the initial crash investigations, the cause was a build-up of ice on the plane's wings and the pilot was found culpable. After a ten-year campaign to clear his name, it was established that the real culprit was an accumulation of slush at the end of the runway, which critically reduced the plane's take-off speed.

Twenty-one people, including seven Manchester United players, were killed outright. They included the team's captain, Roger Byrne, and five of the previous year's Cup Final team. An eighth player, Duncan Edwards, died in hospital two weeks later. Manager Matt Busby's life hung in the balance for several weeks, before his eventual recovery. Among those killed was former England goalkeeper, Frank Swift, who had gone on to work as a journalist for the *News of the World*. He was one of eight journalists killed in the accident.

There was a national outpouring of grief for the team. A disaster fund attracted donations from the length and breadth of the country, and both the eventual European Cup winners, Real Madrid, and United's defeated opponents in Belgrade called for the team to be made honorary European champions for 1958. However, with most of their first team gone, how would the club complete the season? The Football Association agreed to look at waiving the usual rules for registering new players.

Within two weeks, a new Manchester United eleven turned out at Old Trafford for an FA Cup tie against Sheffield Wednesday. Just two of the players who had been in the air crash made their appearance and many were drawn from the club's third or youth teams, some of them playing in unfamiliar positions. One, Stan Crowther, had only been signed from Aston Villa two hours before the game and three of the team were on loan from the non-League club, Bishop Auckland. One of the newcomers, the outside left Shay Brennan, had never played in that position before (he was normally a full-back) and his experience of top-level football until then was limited to three games for the reserves. The inexperienced player scored two of the goals in United's 3–0 win, at the start of a run that would take the rejuvenated club to the 1958 Cup Final (where they lost 2–0 to Bolton).

Matt Busby recovered to return to the manager's job, where he built a second generation of Busby Babes, including the likes of Denis Law and George Best, but with only two of the crash survivors – Bobby Charlton and Bill Foulkes.

Players lost in the Munich air crash:

Geoff Bent
Roger Byrne
Eddie Colman
Duncan Edwards
Mark Jones
David Pegg
Tommy Taylor
'Billy' Whelan

On This Day …

January

4 January 1954 A young truck driver goes into the Sun Recording Studio in Memphis, and pays to cut a demo disc as a present for his mother. Proprietor Sam Phillips is interested in the recording and decides to contact Elvis Presley further.

9 January 1957 Anthony Eden resigns as Prime Minister.

10 January 1956 Sam Phillips sells Elvis Presley's recording contract to RCA for $35,000. In the first year alone, RCA sell 10 million records.

— 1957 Harold Macmillan is appointed Prime Minister.

11 January 1954 All Comet airliners are grounded after a crash in the Mediterranean.

15 January 1958 Campaign for Nuclear Disarmament is formed.

21 January 1950 Author George Orwell dies of tuberculosis.

22 January 1959 Racing driver Mike Hawthorn dies in a road accident.

23 January 1955 Express train crashes at Sutton Coldfield – fourteen dead.

— 1956 Film producer and director Alexander Korda dies.

28 January 1953 Derek Bentley is hanged for the murder of a policeman during a robbery. His conviction is overturned in 1998.

29 January 1959 Dense fog nationwide causes transport chaos.

31 January 1953 Car ferry sinks in the Irish Sea – 130 dead.

— 1956 A.A. Milne, author of *Winnie the Pooh*, dies.

— 1958 America's first satellite, *Explorer I*, is launched, months after Russia's *Sputnik* started the space race.

February

1 February 1952 Television detector vans introduced to catch licence dodgers.

— **1953** Storms along the east coast. Extensive flooding. 307 in total die.

2 February 1955 £212 million programme of highway improvements, including the first motorways, announced.

3 February 1959 Buddy Holly, Ritchie Valens and the Big Bopper are killed in an air crash. Don McLean's song 'American Pie' commemorates it as 'the day the music died'.

5 February 1953 Sweet rationing ends.

6 February 1952 King George VI dies.

— **1958** Munich air disaster – eight Manchester United players among the dead.

7 February 1957 Bill Haley and His Comets arrive at Southampton. Fans go wild.

8 February 1952 Princess Elizabeth is proclaimed queen on her arrival back from Kenya.

— **1955** London Transport announce a new Tube line, from Victoria to Walthamstowe.

11 February 1956 Missing Soviet spies, Burgess and Maclean, turn up in Moscow.

13 February 1958 Christabel Pankhurst, leading light of the suffragette movement, dies.

15 February 1952 George VI buried.

— **1955** Government announces plans to build twelve nuclear power stations over the next ten years.

16 February 1956 MPs vote in favour of abolishing the death penalty.

16 February 1957 The 'Toddlers' Truce' – the one hour break in television transmissions to enable parents to get young children to bed – is ended, and the youth programme *6–5 Special* is slotted into the gap.

17 February 1958 First meeting of the Campaign for Nuclear Disarmament, at Central Hall, Westminster.

18 February 1956 Commercial television broadcasts spread to the Midlands.

— **1957** First broadcast of television magazine programme *Tonight*, introduced by Cliff Michelmore and featuring Cy Grant's topical calypsos.

21 February 1952 Wartime identity cards scrapped.

24 February 1950 General Election – Labour returned with a reduced majority.

— **1955** An extreme freeze across Britain causes chaos.

25 February 1952 Sainsbury's open Britain's first purpose-built, self-service supermarket at Eastbourne.

27 February 1956 Yodelling cowboy, Slim Whitman starts his British tour. His record, 'Rose Marie', tops the domestic charts for eleven weeks, a record that would stand for thirty-six years.

— **1955** Sales of 45 rpm records exceed those of 78s for the first time.

28 February 1953 Watson and Crick announce their discovery of DNA.

March

1 March 1950 Klaus Fuchs is sentenced to fourteen years in prison for spying.

6 March 1951 Actor and composer Ivor Novello dies.

8 March 1950 Rover test the first gas-turbine powered car.

9 March 1950 Timothy Evans is hanged for the murder of his wife and daughter – a crime later attributed to Reginald Christie.

11 March 1955 Sir Alexander Fleming – the discoverer of penicillin – dies.

12 March 1950 Air crash at Cardiff – eighty people killed.

15 March 1949 Clothes rationing ends.

16 March 1950 The *Daily Express* introduces the Gambols cartoon strip, which epitomised middle-class England.

17 March 1952 Wartime utility clothing scheme ends.

— **1957** British European Airways withdraws twenty-five *Viscount 301* aircraft after a fatal accident in Manchester.

24 March 1953 Death of Queen Mary, widow of King George V.

— **1958** Private Elvis Presley – or, as he is to be known, 53310761 – is drafted.

25 March 1957 Treaty of Rome signed, creating a united Europe (without Britain).

27 March 1952 Cheese ration reduced to 1oz a week.

April

1 April 1957 The BBC's most famous April Fools' Day hoax – a report on the Swiss spaghetti harvest.

4 April 1958 First CND Aldermaston march begins.

5 April 1955 Winston Churchill stands down as Prime Minister.

10 April 1957 John Osborne's play, *Look Back in Anger*, opens at the Royal Court Theatre.

12 April 1953 Prime Minister Anthony Eden operated on for gallstones. The operation goes wrong; Eden nearly dies and never fully recovers his health.

— 1954 Bill Haley and His Comets record 'Rock around the Clock'. A possible candidate for the official birthdate of rock and roll?

14 April 1950 The *Eagle* comic is first published.

— 1951 Labour politician Ernest Bevin dies.

16 April 1952 The Queen launches the Royal Yacht, *Britannia*.

17 April 1956 Harold Macmillan's budget includes the introduction of Premium Bonds.

19 April 1956 Navy diver 'Buster' Crabb disappears under mysterious circumstances, and is presumed dead.

21 April 1952 *Watch with Mother* is first seen on television.

— 1952 Labour politician, Sir Stafford Cripps dies.

— 1955 The end of almost a month's strike by newspaper maintenance workers that starved the nation of newspapers (except the *Guardian* – printed in Manchester). Bookmakers' business is badly hit, magazine sales boom and library loans increase.

25 April 1953 Watson and Crick publish a scientific paper describing the structure of DNA.

29 April 1958 *My Fair Lady* opens in London and is a huge hit.

May

2 May 1952 World's first scheduled jet airliner flight. Thirty-six passengers travel from London to Johannesburg in a BOAC Comet.

— 1953 The 'Stanley Matthews' Cup Final, the first one to be televised. Blackpool beat Bolton Wanderers 4–3.

3 May 1951 Royal Festival Hall and Festival of Britain opened.

6 May 1954 Roger Bannister runs the first ever sub-four-minute mile (3min 59.4sec).

7 May 1956 Health Minister R.H. Turton rejects calls for a government campaign against smoking, saying there is no evidence of its harmful effects.

14 May 1957 Petrol rationing (reintroduced in late 1956 during the Suez crisis) is ended.

21 May 1950 A tornado sweeps through the Home Counties – two are killed, others injured.

— 1955 Chuck Berry records his first hit – 'Maybellene'.

22 May 1958 Jerry Lee Lewis' UK tour is cancelled after it is discovered that he has married his thirteen-year-old cousin – while still married to his first wife.

23 May 1954 England footballers beaten 7–1 by Hungary – their worst ever defeat.

25 May 1951 Soviet spies Burgess and Maclean disappear, just as MI5 are about to question them.

26 May 1950 End of petrol rationing.

27 May 1955 General Election – Conservative majority increased to fifty-nine.

28 May 1959 Two monkeys return to earth, and were wrongly said to be the first creatures to survive a trip into space.

29 May 1950 First pilot episode of *The Archers* radio series broadcast.

— 1953 Everest climbed by a Commonwealth expedition led by Colonel John Hunt. New Zealander Edmund Hillary and Sherpa Tenzing Norgay reach the summit.

30 May 1959 Pioneering teenage television programme *Oh boy!* is taken off the air.

June

1 June 1957 Premium Bond prizes are drawn for the first time.

— 1959 First broadcast of *Juke Box Jury*.

2 June 1953 Queen Elizabeth's Coronation.

6 June 1950 First episode of *Educating Archie* broadcast.

9 June 1958 The Queen opens a modernised Gatwick Airport, south of London.

11 June 1955 Huge crash at Le Mans – eighty-four killed.

— 1959 The hovercraft – invented by Christopher Cockerell – officially launched at Southampton.

17 June 1959 Pianist Liberace wins £8,000 damages from the *Daily Mirror* in a famous libel case relating to his sexuality.

23 June 1953 Prime Minister Winston Churchill suffers a severe stroke – its seriousness is not made public.

27 June 1957 The Medical Research Council reports a link between smoking and lung cancer.

29 June 1950 England footballers are beaten 1–0 by part-time Unites States team.

July

4 July 1954 Final rationing – of meat – ends.

5 July 1954 The BBC launches the first television news programme. The news is read by Richard Baker (though the viewers will not have known that, as newsreaders went unnamed and unseen at that time).

5 July 1956 Clean Air Act becomes law.

6 July 1952 The last London tram makes its final trip.

— 1954 First radio broadcast of *Hancock's Half Hour*.

— 1956 First television broadcast of *Hancock's Half Hour*.

— 1957 The Quarrymen 'skiffle' group plays its first gig at a church fête in Liverpool. Their leader is sixteen-year-old John Lennon and in the audience is fifteen-year-old Paul McCartney. The rest is history.

9 July 1955 'Rock Around The Clock' becomes the US number one.

— 1955 First episode of *Dixon of Dock Green* broadcast.

10 July 1956 House of Lords rejects the proposal to abolish the death penalty.

10 July 1958 First parking meters appear in Mayfair, London.

13 July 1955 Ruth Ellis hanged at Holloway Prison.

15 July 1953 Reginald Christie is hanged for the murder of his wife, and held accountable for the murders of at least seven other women.

16 July 1955 Stirling Moss becomes the first Briton to win the British Grand Prix, held at Aintree.

20 July 1957 Harold Macmillan makes his 'never had it so good' speech at Bedford.

23 July 1958 First female peers take their seats in the House of Lords.

— 1957 A provincial bus strike enters its fourth day and turns violent. Buses and their drivers refusing to strike are attacked.

26 July 1956 Colonel Nasser announces the seizure of the Suez Canal.

27 July 1956 Jim Laker takes a record 9 wickets for 90 runs in the Old Trafford test match against Australia.

28 July 1955 Clean Air Bill published.

29 July 1958 America sets up the North American Space Agency (NASA) that will eventually take man to the moon.

30 July 1954 Television Bill becomes law, opening the way for commercial television.

31 July 1959 Cliff Richard gets his first number one hit with 'Living Doll'.

August

4 August 1954 Independent Television Authority set up.

9 August 1958 EMI signs a record deal with a seventeen-year-old Cliff Richard.

12 August 1953 Russians test an atomic bomb.

16 August 1952 Flash floods in Lynmouth, Devon, kill thirty-four people.

— 1959 The Street Offences Act, a product of the work of the Wolfenden Committee, comes into effect. Its aim is to drive prostitution off the streets.

18 August 1959 British Motor Corporation launches the Mini.

19 August 1953 England wins the Ashes for the first time since 1932/3.

— 1959 Pioneering sculptor Jacob Epstein dies.

23 August 1958 First race riots in Nottingham.

27 August 1950 The first television pictures from overseas (Calais) are shown in Britain.

28 August 1952 Vulcan bomber makes its maiden flight.

30 August 1958 Race riots spread to London's Notting Hill.

September

1 September 1958 Cod wars with Iceland begin.

4 September 1957 Wolfenden Report recommends legalising homosexual acts between consenting adults in private. Proposal rejected by Government in December 1957. It also recommends increasing the penalties for prostitutes soliciting.

5 September 1958 End of Notting Hill race riots.

— 1959 The first STD (Subscriber Trunk Dialling) telephone call made from a phone box.

6 September 1952 A de Haviland 110 fighter plane, doing a display at the Farnborough Air Show, breaks up in midair. Thirty-one are killed and sixty-three injured. The rules governing flying displays are tightened.

— 1959 Film actress Kay Kendall dies of leukaemia, aged thirty-two.

9 September 1950 Soap rationing ends.

11 September 1956 Showings of the film *Rock Around the Clock* lead to disturbances in British cinemas.

21 September 1956 Elvis Presley's 'Hound Dog' reaches number two in the pop charts.

22 September 1955 Commercial television starts broadcasting in the London area.

23 September 1951 King George VI is operated on for lung cancer.

25 September 1955 *Sunday Night at the London Palladium* is broadcast for the first time.

26 September 1953 Sugar rationing ends.

— 1955 Fish fingers are sold in Britain for the first time.

30 September 1951 The Festival of Britain closes.

— 1955 Actor James Dean dies in a car accident.

October

3 October 1952 First British atomic bomb test.

— 1952 Tea rationing ended.

— 1959 Postcodes used for the first time.

4 October 1957 Russia launches *Sputnik*, starting the space age and fuelling fears about Russia's missile technology.

8 October 1952 Harrow train disaster – 112 killed.

— 1957 The start of the fire at the Windscale atomic plant in Cumbria.

— 1959 General Election – Conservatives get a 100-seat majority. Among the intake of new MPs is one Margaret Thatcher.

10 October 1957 Fire took hold of the nuclear power plant at Windscale.

16 October 1958 First broadcast of Blue Peter.

17 October 1956 The first of Britain's civil nuclear power stations – Calder Hall in Cumberland – is opened.

20 October 1956 Anglo-French task force sails from Malta for Port Said and the Suez Canal.

25 October 1951 General Election – Conservatives get a majority of seventeen, despite having a smaller share of the vote than Labour.

—1955 Labour MP names Kim Philby as the third man in the Soviet spy ring, under the cover of parliamentary privilege.

31 October 1955 Princess Margaret cancels plans to marry divorcee Group Captain Peter Townsend.

November

2 November 1957 The *New Statesman* publishes an article by J.B. Priestley that will lead to the setting up of the Campaign for Nuclear Disarmament.

—1959 Prime Minister Harold Macmillan opens the first section of the M1.

3 November 1955 Government considers – and rejects – immigration controls.

— 1957 The second Soviet *Sputnik* is launched, containing the dog, Laika.

5 November 1953 Announcement that all rationing is to cease by 1954.

6 November 1956 British troops land in Egypt but stop short of the Suez Canal.

7 November 1953 RAF takes delivery of the first Blue Danube atomic bomb.

8 November 1958 The first UK album chart is topped by the soundtrack from the film of *South Pacific*. The album would top the charts continuously until March 1960, and has a total of 115 weeks at number one.

9 November 1953 Poet Dylan Thomas dies.

11 November 1953 The first broadcast of *Panorama*.

14 November 1952 The first charts for pop music records are published. 'Here in my heart', by Al Martino is the first number one. Vera Lynn has three chart entries.

25 November 1953 England's footballers humbled by a 6–3 defeat by Hungary.

26 November 1953 House of Lords backs the idea of commercial television.

29 November 1956 The Government announces plans for petrol rationing, in the light of the Suez crisis – it leads to panic buying.

December

4 December 1957 Lewisham train crash – ninety-two people killed.

5 December 1958 Britain's first section of motorway – the M6 Preston By-pass – is opened by the prime minister.

— 1958 The first ceremonial Subscriber Trunk Dialling (STD) telephone call is made – by the Queen (surely she has someone to do that sort of thing for her?).

5–9 December 1952 London smog raises mortality rates by 120 per cent.

7 December 1956 Anglo–French withdrawal from Egypt begins.

— 1955 Clement Attlee announces his resignation as Labour Leader.

14 December 1955 Hugh Gaitskell appointed new leader of Labour Party.

14 December 1959 Artist Stanley Spencer dies.

25 December 1957 First televised Queen's Christmas broadcast.

29 December 1956 Elvis Presley has ten entries in the US top 100 at the same time.

Celebrations

*I*n this chapter, we look at two of the big national celebrations that marked the 1950s.

A pat on the nation's back: The Festival of Britain

In 1851, Britain held the Great Exhibition in the Crystal Palace, to celebrate Britain's success as a manufacturer, exporter and colonial power. In 1943, at the height of the Second World War, the Royal Society of Arts suggested that it might be a good idea to mark its centenary, and the notion was picked up by the post-war Labour Government. However, Britain was far from being able to celebrate its pre-eminence among nations in 1951.

We may have been on the winning side in the recent unpleasantness, but the nation was worn-down and nearly bankrupted by the war. The industries that had paid the nation's bills during times of peace had largely been redirected into the war effort, and were struggling to re-establish themselves in changed world markets. Our infrastructure – neglected for years – was in dire need of renewal. Much of the wartime regime of rationing was still in place (and increasingly resented) and almost anything we could manufacture had to go for export, to pay our debts, rather than for home consumption. To add to the troubles, the nation still harboured delusions of empire that would further overstretch its limited resources in the years to come. In short, Britain was sorely in need of a tonic, and the Government decided that a festival would be just the thing. The organisers called it 'One united act of national reassessment and one corporate reaffirmation of faith in the nation's future.'

Others had different ways of describing it. Winston Churchill called it 'three-dimensional socialist propaganda', and large parts of the right-wing press condemned it, first as a luxury an impoverished nation could not afford, and then (often before having seen it) as worthy, dull and bureaucratic. It is certainly true that the Labour Party hoped that it would create a feel-good factor that would do them no harm in electoral terms, and one of Churchill's first acts as a re-elected Prime Minister would be to get the main site cleared.

The primary focus of the festival was an area of the South Bank of the Thames in London, opposite Charing Cross Station. There, a 'Dome of Discovery' celebrated exploration of all kinds, from adventurous trips to the corners of the earth to the nation's achievements in fields like atomic physics. There were many novelties to be marvelled at; some of them now familiar parts of our lives, like escalators, colour television and 3D cinema, but others were technological blind alleys, like Rover's gas-turbine car.

The Skylon, a 292ft-high aluminium cigar, pointed skywards for no obvious reason and lit up at night. Churchill thought it was a Labour party logo and the population at large joked that, like the British economy, it had no visible means of support. This did not stop a student climbing it and tying his scarf around the top, which some poor worker had to retrieve. Britain's industrial achievements were celebrated (coalmining and shipbuilding were featured prominently, which speaks volumes for the nation's post-war economic prospects).

One corner of a pavilion was devoted to that most English of qualities – eccentricity. The organiser of that exhibit, writer Laurie Lee (he of *Cider with Rosie* fame), appealed to the public to come forward with:

> ... something rich and strange, something altogether unheard of; objects, for instance, that are curious and unusual; models constructed of the most unlikely materials, ingenious machines evolved for unpredictable purposes ...

What was entirely predictable was that his appeal would attract everyone on a spectrum from the mildly eccentric to the criminally insane. The organisers found themselves deluged with proposals for concrete top hats, devices that could be screwed onto the backs of chickens to count the number of eggs laid, rubber buses that could be deflated to go under low bridges, and machines for grinding smoke.

The one part of the South Bank Festival complex that was destined to survive the festival itself was the Royal Festival Hall, which by 1988 became a Grade I Listed building – the first post-war structure to be afforded that level of protection. It opened with a concert of English music (at least it did if you counted Handel as English).

'Good' design and Britain's ability to deliver it was at the heart of the Festival's message. Predictably, both the hard-line modernists and the dyed-in-the-wool traditionalists found plenty to complain about in the type of 'modernism-lite' that Hugh Casson and his team came up with, and there is still dispute as to how far the Festival influenced the look of Britain over the next decade. That said, for many ordinary visitors, the bright colours and sleekness of the Festival struck just the right note in a world of post-war drabness. To ensure that visitors without an interest in design had something to complain about, the catering was at first, by general agreement, wildly over-priced. A chicken sandwich was between 2*s* 6*d* (12p) and 3*s* 0*d* (15p), while a sit-down dinner was a full 7*s* 6*d* (37p). The organisers were forced to reduce at least some of the prices.

The South Bank was by no means the only focus of celebration. In Battersea there was the Battersea Pleasure Gardens, which later transformed into the Battersea Funfair and only closed in the 1970s. The Lansbury housing estate in Poplar was paraded as a model housing estate (one of the more obvious bits of Labour propaganda, it included a deliberately jerry-built house to illustrate what an incompetent builder was capable of) and featured an exhibition of town planning, based on the imaginary new town of 'Avoncaster'. South Kensington had an exhibition of science and Glasgow one of industrial power. The festival ship, the aircraft carrier *Campania*, toured the nation's ports with a smaller version of the South Bank exhibition, and a land-based touring exhibition of a hundred lorries did something similar for inland towns and cities.

Then there were the small-scale celebrations organised by individual communities. The village of Trowell in Nottinghamshire was chosen as the official Festival Village. This was no chocolate box settlement. Although it had Saxon origins, the village appeared to have gone steadily downhill for the last millennium. It had no village green and the skyline was dominated by slagheaps and the belching chimneys of an ironworks. The village's three pubs and its coalmine had all closed. When people criticised the choice, as hardly showing the fairest face of British village life, Labour Deputy Leader Herbert Morrison (whose responsibility the Festival was) said it was chosen 'as an example of modern social problems in a village'. In his view, it would encourage places that were not conventionally beautiful to improve their amenities. And what did the good citizens of Trowell do to turn their lives around? They arranged a cricket match in Victorian costume, a performance of a comic opera, *Merrie England,* and organised garden awards and the cleaning of the church clock.

Michael Frayn described the project as an enterprise of 'the radical middle-classes, the do-gooders; the readers of the *News Chronicle*, the *Manchester Guardian* and the *Observer*; the signers of petitions, the backbone of the BBC – the herbivores.'

If anyone was in doubt as to the status the establishment attached to the different parts of the Festival, the King opened the South Bank site, while the opening of the Pleasure Gardens was delegated to Princess Margaret. On the opening day of the Pleasure Gardens, a queue a mile long formed, and it took up to five hours to get in. Once inside, the public found the workers still trying to complete it. Those of a certain age may remember some of the attractions at the gardens; there was an outdoor roller-skating rink, a motor cycle wall of death, a treetop walk and the caterpillar (a ride with the additional frisson of a cover suddenly folding over the passengers' heads). The Rotor ride whirled you around at high speed, pinning you to the sidewall by centrifugal force, before the floor dropped away from beneath your feet. There were dodgems, go-karts, a big dipper and pony rides in the children's zoo, and many younger visitors found magic in the Grotto. Among the sideshows was one where you threw a ball at the target and a direct hit tipped a lady out of her bed (the added bonus for your father being that she was wearing a baby doll nightdress).

One of the greatest attractions in the Festival Pleasure Gardens was a 500-yard narrow-gauge railway, but the Far Tottering and Oyster Creek Branch Railway was no ordinary rail service. It was based on a series of cartoons drawn for *Punch* before the war by Rowland (or Roland) Emmet, depicting a highly eccentric and dilapidated branch line. The supposed engineering of the locomotives was baroque in its complexity. *Nellie* was the only engine that appeared to have started life as any kind of locomotive; *Neptune* appeared to have been built from parts of a paddle steamer, while *Wild Goose* seemed to be second cousin to a hot air balloon. The stations were similarly bizarre, fairy-tale structures. Notices warned visitors not to tease the engines.

By some measures, the FT&OCBR was far more efficient than the state-run, real thing. It carried over 2 million passengers in its short life and recouped its initial cost within just three weeks. It was also an early user of more modern diesel power; war surplus diesel searchlight generator engines provided the traction, long before most of British Railways moved away from steam.

If attendance numbers are a measure of success, the South Bank site did best of the Festival sites, with 8,455,863 visitors. The less cerebral Pleasure Gardens were not far behind, with 8,031,000. The exhibition ship, *Campania*, attracted 889,972 people on its tour, but the People's Architecture exhibit at the George Lansbury estate in Poplar only managed to drag in 86,646 visitors. Perhaps more relevant is the statistic that 58 per cent of those visiting the South Bank came away with favourable impressions. Perhaps even more relevant is the fact that the South Bank's attendance figures were only achieved by them halving the price of evening tickets, and by the Festival site gaining a reputation as an easy place to pick up girls. So much for a 'national reassessment and corporate reaffirmation of faith in the nation's future'.

Coronation

Everybody knows the outcome of the coronation, so instead let's take a sideways look at some of the details of making it happen. The organiser of the event was the Duke of Norfolk in his capacity as Earl Marshal, a post his family had held since 1386, and it was his wife, Lavinia, who was 'crowned' (several times) in the dress rehearsals. The Duke's view of the world had been fixed during his formative years – the 1380s – and much of the coronation ceremony he organised was largely a rerun of those of 1937 and 1910, which had themselves reversed the modernising efforts of Edward VII for his own 1902 coronation.

Indeed, much of the ceremony harked back even further, to the crowning of the first King of England – Edgar, in AD 973. This was despite the despairing efforts of Prince Philip, who chaired the organising committee, to introduce 'some features relevant to the world today'. The throne on which the Queen sat to be crowned was virtually still under warranty (by coronation standards), having first seen duty as recently as 1308 in the coronation of Edward I.

The Duke of Norfolk was an absolute stickler for precedent and protocol, laying down iron rules as to who was invited, where they sat and who wore or did what. This was just as well, since many of the guests (and would-be guests) were similarly obsessed. Lord Mountbatten was one example of someone who was particularly outraged that he was not being given the precedence he felt he deserved in the procession. The question of whether divorcees would be admitted to the Abbey was another of the hotly debated subjects of the day. One somewhat prosaic consideration for the Duke was the toilet arrangements. He rightly recognised that they were fundamental to the success of the day, particularly since the guests had to be in place four hours before the ceremony. Attention to detail included ensuring that the toilets set aside for members of the peerage had seats lined with blue velvet. Not every aspect of the ceremony was clearly laid down, however. In the case of St Edward's crown, there was even uncertainty about which way round it should be worn. At the time of George VI's coronation, someone had tied a thread to it, to indicate the correct way around, but someone else had removed it. Nothing was too obscure to provoke a controversy. Earlier, at the time of the Queen's wedding, there had even been a row over claims that her wedding dress had been made with the assistance of 'enemy' silkworms from Japan. Designer Norman Hartnell had been forced to prove that they were from China, and, therefore, 'our chaps'.

The Coronation of George VI, in 1937, was still relatively fresh in many people's memories and the Government was determined that it should be an equally successful event for the public, both to help revive the country's tourist economy, and so that the (by now Conservative) Government could bathe in its reflected glory for electoral reasons. Churchill had an additional reason for wanting it to succeed – he wanted it to outshine Labour's Festival of Britain, which he had cordially hated. However, the cost of the coronation was a consideration for a cash-strapped government – £1.5 million was set aside for the bill, but this might not have gone far, with a cast list of 29,200 military personnel and 8,000 police involved (many of the latter were camped out in Kensington Gardens).

Another major expense was turning Westminster Abbey into a theatre. Its normal capacity was 2,000, but this had to be increased to over 8,000 to accommodate everyone on the Duke of Norfolk's list. The Abbey was closed to the public from January onwards, as false floors and grandstands were erected within. Even so, many of those attending were able to see little or nothing of the ceremony.

This was the first real media coronation. In 1937, the fledgling television service had just three broadcast cameras outside the Abbey. At first, Princess Elizabeth, the Prime Minister, the Cabinet, and the Church were united in opposition to televising events inside the Abbey. It was argued that the hot lights would make it uncomfortable for everyone, that it would generally add to the stress of the occasion for the Princess, and that live broadcasting meant that any errors would be seen immediately by the public, without any opportunity to edit them out. This initiated a public campaign, led by Lord Beaverbrook and the *Daily Express* (and naturally supported by the BBC), to reverse the decision. It was pointed out that additional lighting would not be needed and when Peter Dimmock, head of outside broadcasts for the BBC, was asked to show the organisers how intrusive television coverage of the ceremony would be he switched the cameras to their most wide-angle lenses, so that the Princess and other key players were tiny dots in the distance.

The Princess was the first person to be convinced by the idea, and Churchill – with his desire to outdo the Festival of Britain – followed. The Archbishop of Canterbury, concerned at televising what was, in effect, a religious service, was one of the last to be convinced. 'But these televisions are everywhere,' he said. 'If the service is televised it will be seen not only by people in their homes but in public houses!' Churchill was able to reassure him (on who knows what authority) that the reception in public houses would be no less reverential than the one they would receive from the great and the good in the Abbey. Permission was eventually given, and the BBC began planning its most ambitious outside broadcast ever, running from 10 a.m. to 11.30 p.m., costing them £44,000 and pressing every camera they possessed into use. There was not even full coverage of a television signal across the country at that time, and the BBC was forced to erect temporary transmitters to fill the gaps. The ceremony planners in the Abbey did not give top priority to the needs of television, and one of their key vantage points was so cramped it could only be used by their very smallest cameraman, a diminutive five-footer named Flanagan. Nonetheless, the huge numbers witnessing the event in their homes had, thanks to the cameras (now switched to telephoto) and the authoritative voice of anchor man Richard Dimbleby, a much better view of what was going on, and a much better idea of what it all signified than most of the dignitaries gathered in the Abbey.

Television coverage of the coronation even intruded into the controversy about the introduction of commercial television in Britain. Opponents of commercial television were able to contrast the BBC's respectful coverage of the event with the American version, which was punctuated by advertisements featuring J. Fred Muggs, a tame chimpanzee dressed in human clothing in the manner later copied by Britain's PG Tips monkeys. Inattentive American viewers may well have ended up wondering what his role in the ceremony was.

Popular wisdom has it that the coronation marked the birth of television as a mass medium. Whilst it is true that it did promote a huge increase in the number of sets (526,000 were sold in 1953 alone), the televised funeral of King George VI the previous year had also been marked by a rapid growth in television ownership. There were only 344,000 licensed sets in 1950, but this had grown to 1,449,000 by the end of 1952. In the event, some 20 million people watched the televised ceremony, compared with the 12 million who listened to it on the radio.

So, the reality was that the television cameras would give a much more intimate view of the ceremony than the BBC had let on. This created an unexpected problem for the Princess. Her chief supporter at the ceremony was Michael Ramsay, then the Bishop of Durham. He was blessed with a pair of extremely hirsute and mobile eyebrows, and the Princess had to ask him to make a supreme effort to keep them still during the ceremony. Otherwise, they were in danger of making her laugh and undermining the solemnity of the occasion.

Of course, coronation merchandising also came into its own. The Design Council had its own informal classification for these items – 'good', 'bad' and 'horrible'. Gathered among the souvenir pencils and teacups there was an item that probably had not appeared at previous coronations – knickers with the Union flag printed on them. They probably fell into a design category of their own – treasonable.

Snappy Dressing – 1950s Fashion

'Why do you have to be a non-conformist – like everyone else?'
(1950s cartoon caption)

*B*ritain in 1950 may have been a country no longer at war, but it was very nearly still a country in uniform. Thousands of young people still found themselves wearing military costume as a result of National Service, but even for those who had served their time, it had merely given way to the uniformity of the relatively small range of choice offered by the demob suit. The constraints of the utility clothing scheme would linger on until March 1952 (clothes rationing ended in 1949). The utility scheme had originally been introduced in 1941 to limit the amount of material and labour devoted to clothing the civilian population during wartime. It brought in a whole range of rules about the design of clothing that bore the utility CC41 mark (no turn-ups on sleeves or trousers, maximum of three buttons and three pockets, skirts 19in from the ground, limits on pleats, a limited range of fabrics, and so on). The Board of Trade brought in some of the nation's top fashion designers – Hardy Amies, Norman Hartnell and others – to design a range of clothing based upon these rules, and even *Vogue* magazine gave it their approval, calling it an 'outstanding example of applied democracy'. However, it did considerably limit the variety on which fashion thrives.

Overseas, things like Christian Dior's post-war, new look made lavish use of materials and innovative craftsmanship, and British shoppers (unless they were very wealthy indeed) could only look on in envy through the pages of the fashion magazines. The upper end of the clothing market did, however, see some small sign of a revival from 1947, when the presentation of debutantes at court was reintroduced. The clothing requirements of the season would far exceed anything that could be supplied through the official rationing scheme.

Itsy bitsy teeny weeny clothes

Some new developments in fashion imposed much less of a demand on materials. The French engineer Louis Reard and fashion designer Jacques Heim were both credited with having invented the bikini (named after the atoll where the Americans held their atomic bomb test) in 1946. The American government may have played a part in encouraging the idea – during the war, their austerity measures included a 10 per cent reduction of the amount of material manufacturers were allowed to use in making women's swimwear. Even so, quite how Reard and Heim can substantiate their claim to invention is questionable, when pre-war vaudeville and burlesque artists were wearing them, something similar existed in both ancient Roman and Greek times, and the earliest recorded bikini-type garment dated back to at least 1,600 BC. One reason for their claim may be that their versions were notably briefer than that of their predecessors. What we can be sure of is that the 1950s was the battleground in which the bikini made its way from the scandalous to something approaching acceptable swimwear.

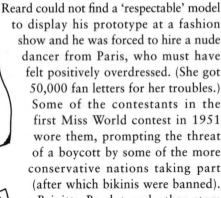

Reard could not find a 'respectable' model to display his prototype at a fashion show and he was forced to hire a nude dancer from Paris, who must have felt positively overdressed. (She got 50,000 fan letters for her troubles.) Some of the contestants in the first Miss World contest in 1951 wore them, prompting the threat of a boycott by some of the more conservative nations taking part (after which bikinis were banned). Brigitte Bardot and other stars endowed them with glamour by wearing them on the beach at the Cannes Film Festival, though neighbouring Spain, Portugal and Italy all banned them, and the Pope declared them sinful. Bardot herself was told by officials on one beach that two-piece bathing suits were not permitted. 'Which piece do you want me to take off?' she asked them innocently. Some magazine editors, confronted by pictures of a woman in a two-piece costume that revealed her navel, would airbrush the offending item out, to make her look as if she had been the product of some immaculate conception.

There was no shortage of people ready to condemn the bikini – and the morals of those who wore them. Even Reard called the bikini 'a two-piece bathing suit which reveals everything about a girl except her mother's maiden name'. As late as 1957, the American magazine *Modern Girl* advised its readers that 'it is hardly necessary to waste words over the so-called bikini since it is inconceivable that any girl with tact and decency would ever wear such a thing.' However, for many people, the fondly remembered moment when the bikini made its transition, at least into the mainstream, if not to respectability, would come in 1962, when Ursula Andress stepped out of the sea in her two-piece in the James Bond film *Doctor No*.

The teenage look

Up until the 1950s there tended not to be recognisably different teenage fashions. Previous eras, such as the mid- to late 1920s had fashions that were youthful, but these were not aimed exclusively at a youth market. By and large, young women wore the same sorts of clothes as their mothers, in the hope of looking more sophisticated. However, as teenagers began to differentiate themselves from their parents' generation through their music and entertainments, so too did separate teenage fashions emerge. Soon, far from daughters dressing like their mothers, mothers were dressing more like their daughters, in fond hopes of being mistaken as one of their daughter's friends. Barbie dolls were marketed as a 'teenage fashion model', something that would have been unthinkable before the war. The emergence of teenage fashions was helped by the manufacturers realising that the real spending power no longer sat with the middle-class, middle-aged matrons of yore, but with younger people.

This differentiation went right down to their nether garments. The corsetry favoured by the more mature lady to contain her ample charms (more civil engineering than lingerie) was rejected by the younger customer, in favour of simpler suspender belts or lightweight, pull-on panty girdles. (The latter became possible thanks to the invention of nylon, and were essential for those ladies without a maid or other willing assistant to lace them up in the traditional variety.) For younger men (particularly, though not exclusively) Y-fronts became a popular choice. They were introduced in 1938, but only generally available post-war.

For sir ... ?

One feature that marked 1950s teenage fashion was its diversity. Just as no individual teenage culture came to dominate the decade, no single fashion code emerged. For the beats, following the dictates of writer Jack Kerouak and jazz musicians like Dizzie Gillespie, the uniform was shades, cord trousers or chinos, a beret and a US surplus flying jacket or duffle coat. Biker fans of Marlon Brando in *The Wild One* adopted his leather jacket and jeans. Those young men looking for fashion role models in the field of popular music may have been equally confused. Few would have gone down the fashion cul-de-sacs blazed by Bill Haley and His Comets, but Elvis both dressed down and up in the course of his career. He started out in the kinds of denim jackets, checked shirts, jeans and boots that he might have worn in his previous career as a trucker, but later graduated to blue suede shoes and the kind of diamante-encrusted excess that, at its worst, almost rivalled Liberace.

The Edwardians ...

The teenage style that epitomised the 1950s was the 'teddy boy'. Shortly after the war, a group of elegant young men-about-town (including a number of ex-Guards officers) started favouring an Edwardian influence in their clothing. It was felt to be dandified, smart and very British. By the early 1950s, this style had been adopted by the ready-to-wear market and began to filter down to working-class customers. On its way, it became somewhat transformed by the addition of elements from the 'zoot suit' and other American trappings (helped in part, it is suggested, by the fashions worn by the West Indian immigrants arriving in this country on the *Empire Windrush* in 1948).

The zoot suit was based on the American riverboat gambler style of dress favoured by Clark Gable in the film *Gone with the Wind*. This became fashionable among Mexican immigrant youths in the southern United States during the war, and developed an association there with criminality, particularly after one of the zoot-suited gangs got involved in a sensational murder. The string tie was another American import that formed part of 'dressing in the Edwardian manner' (the term 'teddy boy' was only coined – as a term of abuse – by the *Daily Express* in 1953). Crepe-soled shoes were also added, probably for jiving, along with the Brylcreemed hair and huge quiff. The whole outfit, if custom-made, could cost £100, or between ten and twenty weeks' wages; it was seen in some quarters to be mildly subversive to appropriate the style of clothing worn by one's social superiors of an earlier generation.

At first, though, the style was relatively classless and had no pejorative overtones, but the teddy boys gradually became very negative figures. Craig and Bentley (*see* Chapter 2) were wearing teddy boy gear when they shot a policeman; a gang of teddy boys committed a nasty murder on Clapham Common in 1954; they were associated with the Rock around the Clock riots and the racially motivated disorder in Notting Hill, in 1959. It did not take long before anyone wearing a teddy boy outfit was automatically branded a trouble-maker and banned from some places of entertainment.

... and the modernists

Towards the end of the decade, around 1958, a group of smartly dressed young men began to emerge, calling themselves 'modernists' to reflect their liking for modern jazz. As the fifties became the sixties, their musical tastes started changing and they started shortening their name to 'mods'. Just as the modernists were making their appearance, John Stephen was opening his first of many shops in what would later become the epicentre of 1960s fashion – Carnaby Street – and Mary Quant was beginning her career as a fashion designer.

For madam ... ?

Young women, looking to the cinema for role models, might have been equally bewildered. Doris Day gave them the girl-next-door look, but the likes of Jane Russell, Marilyn Monroe and Elizabeth Taylor offered a more glamorous and exotic (if not easily replicable) model, while Grace Kelly offered cool sophistication, and Audrey Hepburn elfin delicacy. If all else failed, there was always Hattie Jacques. Meanwhile, female jivers went for flared skirts and underskirts, wide elastic belts, white ankle socks over seamed tan stockings, with hair tied back in a ponytail and flat black pumps. Definitely not for jiving were the new stiletto heels with their winkle-picker toes, which damaged many a 1950s floor and ruined many feet (both of those who wore them and those impaled by standing too close to the wearer). New, easy care synthetic fabrics (nylon, polyester, crimplene) made it a more practical proposition for girls to wear pastel colours and, as the decade progressed, hats tended to go out of style, while trousers became a more acceptable option for many women.

As a (perhaps inevitable) reaction to the wasp waists and conical 'sweater girl' breasts typical of much of 1950s female fashion, the designer Givenchy introduced the shapeless sack dress in 1957, in which even Marilyn Monroe struggled to display the distinguishing marks of her sex. *Time* magazine lamented its arrival, asking, 'Where is the woman?' Givenchy explained that the sack dress:

> … was inspired by modern art, the experimental art that seeks new shapes and forms transgressing the limitations set by convention. I have discarded, among other things, the limitations set by the female figure itself.

To Lucy Noel, the fashion editor of the *Herald Tribune*, this was the end of the world:

> Could it be possible that this is the war of the sexes and that you are about to exterminate woman, just as the praying mantis devours her lover when he has served his purpose? This could ring the end of Homo sapiens as fast as nuclear weapons might do.

So far, humankind seems to have survived the sack dress relatively unscathed. It later evolved into the more enduring styles of the chemise and the shift.

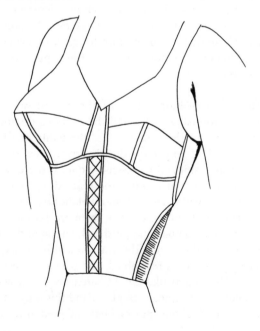

Crimper ... and camper

The 1950s also gave us what was perhaps Britain's first celebrity hairdresser. Raymond Bessone was born in London of French and Italian parents and, after starting out in the business by making wigs and false beards, opened a hairdressing salon in Mayfair – the first of a number across London and elsewhere. These were not cut-price operations – the Knightsbridge salon boasted gilt mirrors and a champagne fountain. Bessone adopted a camp manner, painted his fingernails and spoke with a phoney French accent, and became known as Mr 'Teasy Weasy' Raymond. Stars were drawn to his establishment and found that they could not live without his services, wherever they were. In 1956, actress Diana Dors famously paid £2,500 (at that time, the price of a small house) to fly him to America to give her a shampoo and set. (Mia Farrow would later do the same thing for a $5,000 haircut.)

Raymond had his own television show and was awarded an OBE in 1982. He was also well known for owning racehorses (which included the winner of the 1976 Grand National). Last but not least, he was the inspiration for a future generation of celebrity crimpers, the most famous of his apprentices being Vidal Sassoon.

One other notable hairdresser of the period was Mr Len Pountney of Hounslow, who had the dubious distinction of being reputed to be the originator of the teddy boy hairstyle known as the 'DA' (short for duck's arse), because the rear of the 'do' was fashioned to resemble one. If the DA was the male version of big hair, women too reacted to the utilitarian hairstyles of the war years with more elaborate and romantic coiffures. The 'bouffant' was one of the more extreme of these, with the hair back-combed and piled high on top of the head. As the fifties became the sixties, this found its ultimate expression in the 'beehive', which it resembled, and which was possible by the more widespread availability of hairspray. Sugar water was another method of keeping it in place, and this may have given rise to urban myths about spiders, bugs and even mice taking up residence in them at night. The style was later revived by Amy Winehouse and Marge Simpson.

As an undercurrent to all this diversity, there was still pressure from some quarters to conform to traditional standards. In her 1959 publication *Wife Dressing*, Anne Fogarty advised her readers that:

> … the first principle of wife dressing is complete femininity. It is your husband for whom you are dressing. Blue jeans might be popular in a bachelor girl's wardrobe, but they have no place in a wife's.

And, last but not least, was the change that started to be wrought in clothing shops themselves. For many younger shoppers, the cold formality of the traditional outfitter, with their superior sales staff, was thoroughly daunting. The new model that began to emerge at the end of the fifties had pop music playing, sales staff the same age as their clientele and generally less intimidation of the customer. The age of the boutique was being born.

Right and Proper –
1950s Morality

We tend to think of the 1960s as the decade in which the nation's views on moral matters were transformed, but many of them were live issues in the 1950s. Welcome to the world of 1950s morality and its more interesting alternative, immorality.

Sad to be gay

'Homosexuality in Russia is a crime and the punishment is three years in prison, locked up with the other men. There is a three-year waiting list.'

(Yakov Smirnoff)

'Homosexuals, in general, are exhibitionists and proselytizers and a danger to others, especially the young. So long as I hold the office of Home Secretary I shall give no countenance to the view that they should not be prevented from being such a danger.'

(Sir David Maxwell-Fyfe addressing the House of Commons in December 1953)

The law of the 1950s was somewhat confused in responding to matters of sexual morality. Much of the existing legal framework had been framed in very different times. Adultery and fornication were not offences. Soliciting by prostitutes was an offence, but not the act of prostitution itself. Homosexuality between males was an offence, but not between women. Incest had only fairly recently be deemed a criminal offence.

Being a male homosexual in 1950s Britain was not easy. Homosexuality had been a criminal offence since 1533 and, up to 1861, potentially carried a death penalty. Even in the 1950s, it could still involve a life sentence, and the Home Office after the war had pursued a more vigorous policy of prosecuting offenders. This was not helped by the fact that the two fugitive spies Burgess and Maclean were both known to be homosexual, enabling those who were so inclined to equate homosexuality with a security risk. Over 5,400 cases came before the courts in 1952 alone. In one sensational case in 1954, Lord Montagu of Beaulieu, his cousin Michael Pitt-Rivers and a journalist, Peter Wildeblood, were found guilty of committing homosexual offences with a series of working-class young men, and received sentences of twelve to eighteen months in prison. They were just three of the 1,069 men in gaol for such offences at the end of 1954.

Of equal concern was the use of aversion therapy and hormone treatment to 'cure' offenders. Alan Turing, the wartime code-breaking genius of Bletchley Park, was one of the victims of hormone treatment, which caused one to become impotent and develop breasts, and which was thought to have contributed towards his 'slow descent into grief and madness', resulting in his suicide in 1954. Naturally, the popular press loved to report lurid details of the cases that came before the courts. However, the illegality of homosexuality gave rise to other concerns – such as their vulnerability to blackmail and the police force's use of entrapment to secure convictions.

The Wolfenden Committee was set up in 1954 in the light of all these concerns. It is thought that Home Secretary Sir David Maxwell-Fyfe was hoping for a report that would give him additional ways of controlling homosexuality, but that was not what he would get.

The chairman of the Departmental Committee on Homosexuality and Prostitution was Sir John Wolfenden, a former public school headmaster and at that time Vice-Chancellor of Reading University. His fifteen-man (three of them were actually women) committee included two judges, a Conservative MP, a clergyman, a psychiatrist, a professor of moral theology and a senior Girl Guide. (Am I alone in finding this last choice odd? Surely this is taking 'be prepared' to extremes?) To spare the blushes of his female committee members and secretaries, Wolfenden quaintly insisted that they used the code words 'Huntley' and 'Palmer' instead of the actual 'H' (homosexual) and 'P' (prostitute) words in their discussions. As its title suggests, the committee also had a remit to look at street prostitution but, for the moment, we will focus on what they had to say about homosexuality.

The committee's deliberations took three years – they found it particularly difficult to get evidence from homosexual men who would thus be opening themselves up to potential prosecution, and their evidence had to be disguised behind pseudonyms. Their report was finally published in September 1957. It reflected many of the prejudices of the day and certainly did not find male homosexuality a practice of which they approved – most of the committee actually found it (or, at least, the thought of it) distasteful – but they were more concerned with its relationship to the law. For example, adultery was a sexual practice of which they also disapproved, but in that case, the law did not think it necessary to enforce against it. Two of the important conclusions from their report were that:

> Homosexuality cannot legitimately be regarded as a disease, because in many cases it is the only symptom and is compatible with full mental health in other respects.

> The law's function is to preserve public order and decency, to protect the citizen from what is offensive or injurious, and to provide sufficient safeguards against exploitation and corruption of others ... it is not, in our view, the function of the law to intervene in the private life of citizens, or to seek to enforce any particular patterns of behaviour.

Accordingly, they recommended that homosexual acts between consenting adults in private should no longer be an offence. One member of the committee disagreed with the report and submitted a substantial minority report along with the majority verdict which, once published (it was naturally a best-seller, selling out within hours of going on sale), provoked a lively debate within the country. There was a strong thread of public opinion that was anything but sympathetic to their views, as can be seen from this rant in a 1953 *Sunday Express* column, which apparently attracted a good deal of reader support:

> It is time the community decided to sanitise itself. For if we do not root out this moral rot, it will bring us down as inevitably as it has brought down every nation in history that became affected by it.

> There must be sharp and severe punishment. But more important than that, we must get the social conscience of the nation so roused that such people are made social lepers.

Certainly, Wolfenden's recommendations were too much for the government of the day and it would be another decade before Parliament (prompted by a backbench initiative) substantially implemented the Committee's recommendations on homosexual law reform through the Sexual Offences Act of 1967. One ironic aside to the committee's work is that, during the course of its deliberations, Wolfenden discovered that his own son Jeremy was homosexual.

Prostitution: Ladies of the street

> 'I believe that sex is the most beautiful, natural and wholesome thing that money can buy.'
>
> (Steve Martin)

The other part of the Wolfenden Committee's brief was to look at the law relating to street prostitution. The coronation drew many overseas visitors to Britain, and a number of them commented on the multitude of prostitutes soliciting for trade in certain London streets. American sexologist (a job for which there must have been quite a queue of applicants) Alfred Kinsey did a tour of the West End in 1955 and had no trouble counting a thousand at work. This chimed with complaints from the 'respectable' residents of the streets concerned, who expressed a desire to enjoy the amenities of their neighbourhood without having the outward trappings of vice (so to speak) shoved in their faces (or, in some cases, being badgered by would-be customers). The existing law was, as we have seen, that soliciting was illegal, while prostitution itself was not, but the law on soliciting was clearly not working. It was something that was being more vigorously enforced at the time – the numbers of convictions for soliciting almost trebled between 1946 and 1955 (from 4,393 to 11,878) – but it was not having the desired deterrent effect.

It was not so much the activities of any single prostitute that offended, so much as the volume of trade being done in some areas. In a single Birmingham street, Cheddar Road, there were reputed to be 450 'ladies of the night' plying their trade. Unlike with homosexuality, the Committee did not feel impelled to engage in a philosophical debate about the boundaries between sin and crime. This time, they got on with the job the Home Secretary wanted – recommending ways to be tougher on soliciting. This time, too, the government acted promptly on their recommendations, leading to the Street Offences Act 1959. This provided a system of escalating fines, with the option of a prison sentence for repeat offenders. It also introduced an arrangement that might be described as 'three strikes and you're outed'. Under this, offenders would initially only receive a caution. A third caution within a year meant that you were likely to go to court and the police would be entitled there to label you as a 'common prostitute'.

The Act achieved its narrow aim of substantially reducing the level of street prostitution, but the displaced girls instead filled up the clubs, bars and other locations, which were harder to police; massage parlours, escort agencies and call girls flourished.

Pornography:
Anyone for feelthy postcards?

'Lord Longford asked me what he should do about the
Obscene Publications Bill. I told him straight, I said "Pay it!"'
(Eric Morecombe)

The real impact of the changed moral climate in post-war
Britain was to come in the 1960s, with landmarks like the *Lady
Chatterley's Lover* trial to test out the new Obscene Publications
Act. However, the groundwork for this new liberalism was done
in the 1950s. At this time, the main law relating to pornography
was still the Obscene Publications Act of 1857. The Act itself
did not address the difficult question of what was obscene, but
an important later judgement concluded that obscene material
was likely 'to deprave and corrupt those whose minds are open
to such immoral influences and into whose hands a publication
of this sort may fall'. It can thus be seen as a law primarily to
protect the young and other impressionable groups.

At the time the law was passed, the then Lord Chief Justice gave
Parliament an assurance that a deliberate intention to corrupt the
morals of youth was a vital part of the law, but that was not how
the law (as interpreted by an important later judgement) came to be
applied. It was used in some decidedly dubious ways over the years
– such as preventing the working classes from gaining information
about contraception or human physiology (such as revealing that
women can have orgasms), or prosecuting an exhibition on human
anatomy. There had been efforts for years to get the law changed
and, in 1955, Roy Jenkins brought a Private Members' Bill before
the House, designed to provide a replacement for the Act of 1857.
Despite the support it got in the House, pressure of other business
meant that the new Obscene Publications Act did not find its way
onto the statute book until 1959.

The new Act had some important features. First, it allowed a
defence that a work was 'in the interests of science, literature,
art or learning'. Second, it allowed the admission of expert
evidence to support (or deny) the literary or other merits of

the book. Third, the book had to be taken as a whole – it was not enough (as the prosecution in the Lady Chatterley case had tried to do) to focus on a few mucky bits from it (sorry, I meant explicit passages – we're talking about serious literature here) and condemn the rest of the work by association. Fourthly, the author and publisher could speak in court in defence of the work, even if they had not been summoned. Finally, the new Act made it clear that there had to be an intention to corrupt and deprave the reader. This important new legislation would provide the context for the Lady Chatterley and other high-profile trials in the following decades, and made an important contribution to the more open and tolerant (or disgustingly permissive, depending upon your point of view) society that was to emerge.

'Do you like Kipling?
I don't know, you naughty boy, I've never kippled!'
> (Caption to a McGill postcard that sold a record 6 million copies).

There was one rather curious prosecution in the 1950s that pre-dated the 1959 Act, and which aimed to clarify the boundaries of propriety in a very different medium. The seaside comic postcard had been part of the British way of life since the 1860s, selling some 16 million copies a year at its zenith. Its bawdy humour is part of a comedic tradition that stretches from Geoffrey Chaucer to Benny Hill.

However, was it safe for the lower orders (who were the main customers for them) to be exposed to such lewdness? Council Watch Committees up and down the country thought not, and laid down gloriously inconsistent rules about what could or could not be sold at the end of their particular pier. The councillors at Skegness even lumbered their poor old police with powers to prosecute if, in their view, a particular card gave rise to 'unnatural and lustful desires' (they did not say on whose part – did 1950s police officers have unnatural and lustful desires?). In any event, the local bobbies were unable to advise the representative of the card company who called in on them for advice. The police in Blackpool (where the Council's censorship committee continued meeting well into the 1960s) found a way of delegating this responsibility to the retailer. They would show the stallholder the suspect card and ask 'Would you send this card to your daughter?' If they said 'No', it was considered *prima facie* grounds for a prosecution.

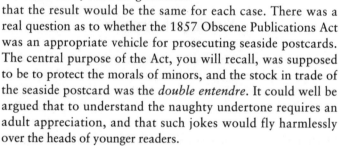

One of the consequences of this localised enforcement of morality was that the poor card manufacturer could face repeated prosecutions relating to the same card, with no guarantee that the result would be the same for each case. There was a real question as to whether the 1857 Obscene Publications Act was an appropriate vehicle for prosecuting seaside postcards. The central purpose of the Act, you will recall, was supposed to be to protect the morals of minors, and the stock in trade of the seaside postcard was the *double entendre*. It could well be argued that to understand the naughty undertone requires an adult appreciation, and that such jokes would fly harmlessly over the heads of younger readers.

Prosecution of postcard manufacturers had gone on for years, but there had been a very light touch under the post-war Labour Government – just 297 postcards were destroyed in 1950. The incoming Conservative Government took a very different view; they were concerned at the nation's declining moral standards, of which the seaside postcard was, in their view, one manifestation. They encouraged a more vigorous enforcement of the law and the number of cards destroyed rose to 11,662 in 1951, increasing to 16,029 and 32,603 in the following two years. It was in 1953 that they decided to go after the doyen of the seaside postcard.

In a career stretching from 1904–62, Donald McGill designed some 12,000 postcards which sold 200 million copies. He created a whole world of weedy husbands, fat, bullying wives, single people who were variously (according to sex) incurably lustful or improbably voluptuous, comic drunks and naïve vicars. In 1953, Lincolnshire Police raided outlets in Skegness and the Director of Public Prosecutions authorised the Chief Constable of Lincolnshire to prosecute McGill's publishers. McGill, by now seventy-nine and in poor health, went to court intent on defending his creations, but was badly advised by his defence and ended up pleading guilty to obscenity in relation to four of his cards and agreeing not to republish seventeen others. He was fined £50, but the loss of income, as nervous retailers decided not to restock, was greater still. Today, his reputation is entirely restored. His comic characters have featured alongside the Queen's head on postage stamps and his original artwork appears in art galleries fetching thousands of pounds.

Sunday observance

'Six days shall work be done, but on the seventh day there shall be to you an holy day, a Sabbath of rest to the Lord: whoever doeth work therein shall be put to death.'

(Exodus 35:2)

'If Britain has not been invaded since 1066 it is because foreigners dread having to spend a Sunday there.'

(A French view of the English Sunday of the 1950s)

Most people old enough to remember the British Sunday of the 1950s will wince at the recollection. Tony Hancock built a whole episode of his comedy programme around the excruciating boredom of it. It was the day on which the most suicides occurred and there was a form of mental illness named after it. We will look at a few aspects of the 1950s British Sunday, and the background to them. The Britain of the 1950s was already a lot less religious than in earlier times – only 13 per cent of the population attended church on a weekly basis in 1952 and by 1954, 60 per cent said they did not attend church at all. However, new arguments had been marshalled for keeping Sunday 'special':

✳ the need to maintain peace and quiet for those who wanted a day of rest, in every sense of the word

✳ the need for a family day, to reinforce family values

✳ the need to avoid the exploitation of workers, who might be pressured into working on a Sunday

✳ that, if Sunday became a day like any other, it would disadvantage the dwindling band who wished to devote their Sabbath to religious activities

One of the first things a modern time traveller to the 1950s would notice is that nearly all of the shops were shut. This was the result of the Shops Act 1950, which imposed strict, if bewilderingly complicated, rules about what could or could not be sold on a Sunday. A few of the apparent anomalies will help to illustrate the problem:

✳ you could buy fast food, but not fish and chips

✳ you could buy bicycle spares, but not a complete bicycle (unless, presumably, you bought it all as spares and assembled it yourself)

✳ you could have your shoes repaired, but could not buy a new pair of shoelaces if one broke

✳ you could sell milk or cream, including clotted cream, but not tinned cream (unless it was clotted)

✳ fresh fruit sales were allowed, but not tinned

There were also rules regarding refreshments, so you could buy a raw kipper, since it could be consumed on its own, but flour and tea need further preparation, so did not count as refreshments and had restrictions on their sale.

All clear so far? Even judges found the rules utterly confusing. As one put it:

> I have found it quite impossible to arrive at any conclusion as to what was in the mind of those who put in this list of those things that may be sold on Sundays, unless it amounts to ... whenever you can think of anything which people are likely to want on Sunday, then a shop may be kept open for that purpose.

We have not even started on the other religious groups yet. Jewish shopkeepers, who already closed on their own Sabbath, would have found themselves at a disadvantage if they also had to close on the Christian day of rest. They had to obtain a certificate of conscientious objection from their Board of Deputies to enable them to open on a Sunday.

The result of all this was a huge amount of breaching of the legislation, with businesses either finding ingenious ways of opening 'without opening' – by way of remaining within the law – or brazenly flouting the rules. The latter was made easier by the fact that the Act only allowed a maximum fine of £1,000, which was relative chicken feed to some of the bigger operators.

The law was promoted by an unholy alliance of religious interests, trade unionists that wished to protect their members against exploitation, and small businesses (and their largely Conservative friends in the House of Commons) who feared commercial disadvantage against their larger rivals, who would be better able to open on Sundays. Of all the liberalising changes that would come forward during this period, this would prove to be the most difficult one to crack. Not even Margaret Thatcher could do it. No less than twenty-nine attempts were made to revise the Shops Act 1950 before the compromise of the 1994 Act found its way onto the statute book.

The choice of Sunday leisure activities was also constrained by a variety of legislation, some of it very archaic. One of the more bizarre pieces was the Sunday Observance Act of 1625, which made it illegal to assemble outside of your parish to play sport.

Although it was not rigorously enforced by the 1950s, it was not actually repealed until 1969. Had it been applied, one of those in trouble might have been the Duke of Edinburgh, who came under fire from the church for playing polo and cricket on a Sunday. The Archbishop of Canterbury, no less, complained that he (the Duke) encouraged 'all who constantly seek to evade the domesticity of Sunday rest and recreations'. The press debate that sprang up around this helped to form a more liberal climate of opinion towards Sunday sport. Even so, in 1953 an attempt by Labour MP John Parker to increase the choice of Sunday entertainment was heavily defeated in Parliament, and Prime Minister Winston Churchill rejected his proposal for a Royal Commission into the matter. A Gallup poll at the time suggested that the majority were opposed to professional sport being played on a Sunday.

Even a national institution like the Festival of Britain fell foul of the 1625 and 1780 Sunday Observance legislation, and a special Act of Parliament was required to enable it to open on Sundays. Even then, both the Lord's Day Observance Society and some of the more mainstream churches opposed the opening of the Pleasure Gardens. The Methodists said:

> The Sunday opening of the amusement park would be utterly contrary to the best traditions of British life, which it is one aim of the Festival to present, and we are therefore resolutely opposed to it.

MPs who favoured the Sunday opening of the more worthy South Bank site, but not of the Pleasure Gardens, were accused of having one law for the rich and another for the poor. However, this did not stop future Speaker George Thomas, reminding the House about the sleazy types who hung around in fairgrounds, or Colonel Wigg (Labour for Dudley) recounting how, some years before, a fairground in Blackpool had exhibited an unfrocked clergyman in a barrel. Sunday opening of the South Bank was approved by Parliament, but not that of the Pleasure Gardens.

For many years, the BBC had done its best to lower the spirits of its listeners with its worthy, but deadly dull, schedule of Sunday radio broadcasting. It was only from the 1930s that they started admitting anything of a secular nature into their programming (and this in the face of stern opposition from the likes of the Lord's Day Observance Society). By the 1950s, part of their daytime radio output on a Sunday was positively jolly, with *Two-Way Family Favourites*, the *Billy Cotton Band Show*, *Life with the Lyons*, *The Navy Lark* and *Beyond our Ken* (which became *Round the Horne*). This last example was perhaps the most surprising addition to the Sabbath schedule, given the (for the time) filthy innuendos contained in the exchanges between the programme's unambiguously gay couple Julian and Sandy. The only explanation can be that neither the BBC executives nor the listeners understood Polari (the slang with which Julian and Sandy spoke).

With television, the real impetus for change at the BBC came with the launch of commercial broadcasting. In its very first week, Sunday nights were for the next decade or more transformed by the launch of *Sunday Night at the London Palladium,* which would become the focal point of many people's Sunday viewing. The *Palm Court Orchestra* simply could not compete.

With live entertainment, the position was legally more complicated. The Sunday Entertainments Act 1932 allowed cinemas to open, subject to conditions relating to staff working hours and payments to the Cinematograph Fund. However, God-fearing people might still think twice about being seen entering them. It also allowed musical entertainments at a licensed venue (straightforward enough, you might think, but what constituted 'a musical entertainment'? Did, for example, the inclusion of an element of comedy or fancy dress override the musical content?) It also allowed for the Sunday opening of museums, galleries, gardens and lectures or debates. However, the jollity did not extend to the licensing of public dancing on the Sabbath. From 1951, the police perhaps wisely decided to leave the prosecution of breaches of the Sunday entertainments rules to private litigants.

Transports of Delight: Getting About in the 1950s

*T*he fifties saw many changes in the way we all got around. New technologies were applied to rail and air travel, and car ownership gradually became something within the reach of most families. In this chapter, we look at some of those changes.

Vickers Viscount

For many people of a certain age, their first experience of flying will have been in the Vickers Viscount, Britain's most successful airliner. It was one breakthrough for 1950s British technology that enjoyed a relatively untroubled life. Its origins lay in the wartime Brabazon Committee, who were asked to assess Britain's post-war air transport needs. They were anxious to catch up on the lead the United States had established in designing transport aircraft. They invited tenders for an aircraft to serve less heavily trafficked routes, their original requirement being that it should carry twenty-four passengers up to 1,750 miles at a cruising speed of

200mph – a replacement for the Douglas DC3 Dakota. It was originally intended to be a conventional piston-engined aircraft, but one of the tenderers, Vickers, felt that this was a technological blind alley and asked to make their proposal a turboprop. The Government accordingly set up two separate tenders.

British European Airways had lobbied for a larger carrying capacity since the beginning and the initial proposal from Vickers did indeed prove to be too small and too slow to be viable. Companies were instead placing orders for the piston-engined option. However, the advantages of turboprop engines were starting to become clear and the Ministry of Supply commissioned a stretched version with more powerful engines, and it was this that first flew from Brooklands, Surrey, in August 1950. The world's first scheduled turboprop entered service with BEA in April 1953. It was an immediate success – quieter, faster and able to fly higher than its conventional rivals were. In all, some 445 of them were built and sold to airlines throughout the world. At times, there was such a waiting list that airlines were forced to go and buy an (inferior) alternative product.

The plane's track record was not entirely without blemish, however. In March 1957, a BEA flight from Amsterdam was coming in to land at Manchester Airport when it went out of control and ploughed through a house in Wythenshawe. All twenty people on board and two people in the house were killed. The air accident investigation found the cause to be metal fatigue in a bolt that held the wing flaps on. BEA withdrew all its Viscount fleet for precautionary checks, but they were back in the air within a week. By a supreme irony, the house destroyed belonged to one of the area's leading campaigners for airport safety. He was so concerned about the situation that he was in the process of buying a property well away from the danger zone. Sadly, his wife and two-year-old son died in the crash.

This would not be the last Viscount crash. Between 1957 and 1974, 398 people were killed in 12 separate accidents, though none of them identified problems serious enough with the plane to ground them in the long term. BEA continued to use them until 1985 and they carried passengers for other airlines until 1997. In 2010, some sixty years after the prototype Viscount flew, one example was still operating in Africa.

The De Havilland Comet

It was the sexiest product of the 1950s British aviation industry, but was proof that it is not always a good idea to be a world leader in the development of technology.

In 1943, the Brabazon Committee identified a need for a pressurised transatlantic mail plane, capable of carrying a 1-ton load at 400mph. The aircraft manufacturer Geoffrey de Havilland sought to persuade them that this should be a turbojet. Conventional wisdom at that time was that jet engines were too unreliable and too thirsty, but he won the argument. The outcome was the de Havilland Comet, the prototype of which first flew in July 1949. The British Overseas Airways Corporation, and the British South American Airways ordered fourteen for delivery in 1952.

Initially, de Havilland faced the problem that the engines they had to use as a stop-gap were underpowered for the load they were supposed to lift. One of the ways they got round this was by using new alloys and other materials on the plane, and new ways of joining them together – gluing them, rather than riveting. They also saved weight by using thinner sheets of metal than was customary. However, by the time the first production models were ready, in 1952, they looked to be onto a winner. It was a world leader – the world's first jet airliner, and it looked sleek with its large square windows. It was 50 per cent faster than the competition of the day and could fly over the bad weather that others were forced to plough through; they were cheap to maintain and fuel efficient at over 30,000 feet. They could even make money with just a 42 per cent passenger loading. The maiden flight, from London to Johannesburg, left on 2 May 1952 and the first passengers loved it.

However, on 26 October 1952, a Comet taking off from Rome crashed. Nobody was seriously hurt, it was put down to pilot error and little more was thought of it. The same thing happened again, at Karachi on 3 March the following year, this time killing all those on board the plane. Again, pilot error was seen as the culprit. Within two months, a third Comet was seen falling from the sky, wingless and on fire, six minutes after taking off from Calcutta. It would require a bad case of pilot error to explain that one. In fact, it had hit a thunder squall; structural failure was blamed and modifications were ordered to all the planes. This did not stop de Havilland from taking up a sizeable number of the Royal household (including the Queen, the Queen Mother and Princess Margaret) on a pleasure flight in one that same June. On 10 January 1954, yet another Comet crashed, this time into the Mediterranean off the island of Elba, twenty minutes out from Rome's Ciampino Airport. By now, BOAC were forced to ground their fleet, while as much as possible of the plane was recovered from the sea and an inquiry looked for the causes of the crash. No fault could be found with the plane and, not least because of the national prestige tied up in the project, the Government decided no further inquiry was needed and flights were resumed.

It was the wrong answer. Shortly afterwards, on 8 April, another Comet went down, this time near Naples and again with all hands on board. This time, they were all grounded, the plane's certificate of airworthiness was withdrawn and production of them halted. The Cohen Committee was set up to enquire exhaustively into all of the Comet crashes. They would be advised by the Royal Aircraft Establishment, and the Royal Navy helped in the painstaking work of recovering the airliner from the sea. Their conclusion was metal fatigue, partly resulting from the new materials and construction techniques, coupled with some design faults (the large square windows had to be replaced by smaller oval ones). De Havilland learned the lessons from the inquiry's detailed work and the result was the Comet 4, which BOAC finally put onto the transatlantic run on 4 October 1958.

It was much improved, but the opposition had caught up and overtaken them in the meantime. That same month, rival airline

Pan Am introduced Boeing 707s onto the same route. They, and the Douglas DC8 which soon followed, were larger, faster, longer-range and cheaper to run than the Comet. BOAC soon switched to the American rival and by 1965 had withdrawn its Comet fleet. The plane continued in service with other airlines until the end of 1981 and a military version, the Nimrod, was not retired until 2011. They flew well enough, but were never big-sellers.

The Comet was, as aviation writer Bill Withun put it, state-of-the-art pushed beyond its limits. Today, it is remembered as much for the advances in air accident investigation it prompted, as for its own technical merits. Britain became a world leader in deep-sea salvage operations and reconstruction techniques as a result of the work carried out on the Comet crashes. Rivals also learned from Comet's design mistakes – Boeing and others hung their engines in pods below the wings, rather than inside them, not least to minimise catastrophic wing damage if the engine caught fire.

The British sportscar

It is difficult to identify one car that epitomises the 1950s British car industry. One of the industry's main problems was the bewildering variety of different makes and models that militated against the economies of scale from which its rivals benefited. The problem was not evident in the early post-war years of worldwide consumer shortages, when virtually any car that could be manufactured would find a ready market. In Britain, with its bankrupt economy, that market had to be primarily overseas. At least 66 per cent, and in some cases up to 90 per cent, of the British car industry's output had to be exported under government rules, and some of our most popular (and fondly remembered) exports were our sports cars.

Initially, the cars that British manufacturers produced were continuations or developments of pre-war models. However, one that most decidedly was not made its debut at the Motor

Show in 1948. Jaguar wanted to showcase the new engine it had developed for the Mark VII saloon. What they did not yet have was a Mark VII saloon to put it in, so, just weeks before the show, their designers were instructed to come up with something. The result was a beautiful, hand-built aluminium sports car body, which, with a 120mph top speed, was faster than any production car then on the market. It went on display at the ridiculously low price of £998, and Jaguar was surprised when a long queue of would-be customers formed. They realised that they had given no real thought to putting it into mass production. It had to be re-engineered more or less from scratch, and the result was the Jaguar XK120. It and its successor, the XK140, continued in production throughout the 1950s and the engine formed the basis for their Le Mans winning racing cars, the C- and D-types.

Standard Triumph wanted a sports car to break into the American market. After an unsuccessful attempt to buy the Morgan Company they decided to build their own. Their first attempt, using a cocktail of spare parts from various Triumph models (including the chassis from a pre-war Standard saloon that they happened to have lying around the factory and the engine that powered, among other things, the Ferguson tractor) was the 20TS. It was essentially based on something put together by an amateur enthusiast and it went on display – without much development – at the Motor Show of 1952. The company gave it to BRM test driver Ken Richardson for his assessment. He did not mince his words, telling them it was a 'death trap' and 'frankly ... the most bloody awful car I've ever driven'. Standard Triumph promptly hired him to improve it. The result, which first appeared at the Geneva Motor Show in 1953, was the TR2. It and its successor, the TR3, would enjoy a good deal of rally success and they would sell some 83,000 of them between 1953 and 1962.

The sports car maker MG was still building what were essentially their pre-war models (in terms of looks and performance) by 1952. They were desperate to introduce a more up-to-date model, but fell victim to corporate politics. They had just become part of the British Motor Corporation who were about to launch their new Austin Healeys and did not want anything coming forward to clash with that. MG were, therefore, forced to soldier on with revamps of the old models until 1955, when they were finally allowed to go ahead with their first modern sports car, the MGA. Its body was based on a car they had entered in the 1951 Le Mans race, and the engine was that used in the Magnette sports saloon. It continued in production until 1962, by which time over 101,000 of them had been sold.

During the early 1950s, the partnership between Donald Healey and BMC had specialised in producing larger, more muscular sports cars, whose market niche fell somewhere between the TR2 and the Jaguar XK120. Healey was then asked to come up with a small, inexpensive sports car, using as many parts as possible from existing BMC models. The result was the Austin Healey Sprite of 1958, in which most of the running gear came from the Morris Minor or Austin A35. Despite these 'donor' cars not having the greatest of sporting pedigrees, the Sprite handled well and had a successful racing career. Its most distinctive feature – the headlamps fixed to the top of the bonnet, giving it the nickname of 'Frog-Eye' – was not Healey's original intention. He had originally wanted to have pop-up headlamps, to give better aerodynamics, but cost considerations forced fixed headlamps on him. This version only continued in production until 1961, but it and its successors (including the MG versions) eventually sold 356,000 cars.

The Mini

Although it is forever associated in the popular consciousness with the swinging sixties, the Mini was conceived and introduced in the 1950s. In fact, the inspiration for it goes back much further – to 1923 and the original Austin 7. This was intended to be an alternative to the motorcycle and sidecar in both size (it was originally designed to have no bigger footprint than a motorcycle combination) and price (it initially sold for £165 – cheaper than any car, other than the mass-produced Ford Model T).

The Mini itself was conceived in 1953 by Alec Issigonis, creator of the Morris Minor, who initially drew the concept of the car on a tablecloth. By the 1950s, bubble cars and mini cars had become an alternative to conventional motoring for the impecunious. British Motor Corporation Chairman Sir Bob Lord hated them. He said, 'God damn these bloody awful bubble cars! We must drive them out of the streets by designing a proper miniature car.'

The car was not actually commissioned until March 1957, by which time the petrol shortage brought about by the Suez crisis had made bubble cars an even more popular choice – sales of small cars quadrupled between 1956 and 1957. The Mini was a remarkably innovative piece of engineering. It was just 10ft 2in long – 2ft 4in less than the Morris Minor – but managed to have more interior space. At first this was going to be achieved by having just a two-cylinder engine, which they made by sawing an Austin A35 engine in half, but this proved to be both rough and gutless, leading to the innovative transverse engine and front wheel drive arrangement that has now become the standard for small cars. Everything about it was new, right down to the tiny 10in wheels (a size more commonly associated with wheelbarrows) that required Dunlop to develop special tyres.

Issigonis' approach to design was certainly pragmatic. He simply plonked four car seats down on the factory floor, got employees of different sizes to sit in them, then worked out how much space they needed around them to do the things one does in a car. The sizing of the door pockets was apparently based on the need for them to hold a bottle of gin. The prototype came together very quickly and, in July 1957, Sir Bob was driven round the Longbridge works in it. His reaction to it was immediate – he told Issigonis to have it ready for production in a year. The performance of the car was a revelation. It cornered as if on rails and the prototypes were capable of over 90mph – this was unheard of in a small car of the day, and they had to tame it by reducing the size of the engine. The Ferrari designer Aurelio Lampredi was lent a pre-production model and even he was bowled over by it, saying, 'If it wasn't so ugly, I'd shoot myself.' In fact, the austere looks of the prototypes did not win everybody over. BMC Managing Director George Harriman was less than impressed – 'What a bloody mess! We'll never sell that! Spend another few quid on it Alec and jazz it up a bit. Put some chrome plate on it or something.'

There were, however, a number of problems with it. First, it was incredibly crude, with sticky sliding windows and doors that opened by pulling a string. Second, like so many products of the British car industry, it was under developed from being rushed into production and suffered from problems such as oil leaks, a rather crunchy gearbox, and both the engine and the passenger compartment getting flooded out in rainy conditions. Thirdly, BMC sold them initially at under £500, including purchase tax. Their rivals, Ford, bought one and took it to pieces, and were at a loss as to how BMC could make a profit on them at that retail price. The answer was that they could not – Ford estimated that BMC were making a loss of £30 on each one they sold. Last but not least, they were also rather dangerous; a Department of Transport study found that it was one of the two small cars in which you were most likely to be injured, in the event of an accident. Not that this worried Issigonis, whose attitude was, 'I make my cars with such good brakes, such good steering that if people get into a crash it is their own fault.'

The public loved them. Not just the impecunious, but royalty (of both the monarchy and the pop music varieties) flocked to buy them. Production continued until 2000, by which time some 5.3 million had been sold (1.5 million of which sold in Britain). In 1995, *Autocar* voted it the car of the century.

Mad and bad – bubble cars and mini cars

Miniature cars have been a part of motoring since the earliest days of the car. Intrepid Victorian passengers would sit between the front wheels of a Léon Bollée Voiturette, their legs protruding out in front to form what we would nowadays call the 'crumple zone'. Europe saw a revival of interest in them in the 1950s, as nations that had been shattered and impoverished by war looked for cheap ways to get mobile again. In Britain, lightweight, three-wheeled cars had low fuel consumption, qualified for lower purchase tax, cheaper road fund licence and insurance, and required only a motorcycle licence, which was very handy for anyone who found car tests a problem.

The 1950s mini cars took various forms. The actual bubble cars took their name from their perspex aircraft-type canopies, which lifted up for the passengers to get in. These were favoured by former German aircraft manufacturers Messerschmitt, who were debarred from aircraft manufacture after the war. With their fore and aft seating, the Messerschmitt could be sold throughout Europe without having to worry about left- or right-hand drive options. It was originally designed as an invalid car and was more like a scooter than a car to drive, with handlebars in place of a steering wheel, a twist-grip throttle and hand-operated clutch. Only the brakes required a foot. One drawback with them was that the canopies worked like a greenhouse and they could become unbearably hot in summer. Some of them, however, did give a respectable performance –

one Messerschmitt set a 24-hour reliability record for vehicles under 250cc at the Hockenheim circuit, averaging 64mph. For those favouring a short but exciting life, there was a four-wheeled version, unofficially named the Tiger (unofficially because Krupps had patented the name for their Nazi tanks). This had a 493cc engine and a 75mph performance, significantly in excess of its handling and braking capabilities.

In Italy (and elsewhere under licence) they built the Isetta. This (and other models like it) had side-by-side seating for the driver and their passenger, accessed by a single front door. Their short length (7ft 6in) meant that they could be parked sideways on to the kerb. But if that kerb was too high, or you parked too close to another vehicle (or they too close to you), you could not open the door – a particular problem if you were inside and your model was not fitted with a reverse gear.

Britain had (among others) the Bond Minicar, developed by an eccentric former aircraft engineer, Laurie Bond. The specification for the original model, which was sold until 1950, was rudimentary to the extreme, including:

❋ a 122cc engine (too small even for a modern lawn mower)

❋ no reverse gear

❋ no rear suspension, except for the flexing of the tyres

❋ steering operated by a system of cables and pulleys

❋ rear-wheel brakes only

❋ perspex windscreen and manually operated windscreen wipers

❋ no driver's door (the opening for a door would have compromised the monocoque construction)

❋ starting on some models involved pulling a rope under the dashboard

The Bond Minicar continued in production until 1966, gradually upgrading its specification until the last models had a pulsating 247cc engine and they were capable of a heart-stopping 51mph flat out.

By the end of the 1950s, the best days of the mini car and bubble car were over. The mainstream motor industry had responded to their challenge by producing more affordable small cars (like the Mini in England and the Fiat 500 in Italy) and growing affluence meant that many more families could afford to own such cars.

The twilight of the railways

So, we have seen that the aviation industry of the 1950s was moving (with varying degrees of success) into an era of new technology, and the roads were steadily filling up with traffic. What was happening meanwhile on the railways? In short, they were being run into the ground.

The problems go back at least as far as the Second World War. It has been argued that the wartime British government inflicted more long-term damage on the railways than the Luftwaffe was ever able to manage, through the overwork and under-investment they imposed on the network. As an asset, the rail network lost about £440 million of its value (at 1948 prices) between 1938 and 1948, mostly due to neglect. By 1946, they had £30 million of air-raid damage and £151 million in arrears of maintenance to contend with, even before any modernisation was considered.

The incoming Labour Government had been committed, since 1908, to rail nationalisation (which finally took place at the start of 1948) but it is doubtful whether any government could have done much else. If re-privatised, the government would have had to compensate them for their renewals fund (£147 million, confiscated during the war) and for all or part of the £1 billion of free services the wartime railways had provided. A cash-strapped Conservative Government in 1948 (had there been one) would have been little more able than Labour to afford these payments.

On the continent, other nations were using the opportunity provided by the rebuilding of their shattered railways to move from steam to diesel or electric traction. No such move was made in Britain. The capital investment needed for electrification could not be afforded, as the Government struggled to build a fledgling National Health Service and meet its other commitments. A move to diesel would have been cheaper and it would even have been possible to convert existing steam locomotives from coal to diesel, but in the days before we discovered North Sea oil, even the running costs of importing the diesel would have been too much for the ailing balance of payments. Britain was underlain by huge deposits of coal, so we went on building steam locomotives (over 2,500 of them under nationalisation) right up until 1960, the last of which would see barely a handful of years of service before the inevitable switchover took place.

Under Labour, the railways would be part of an integrated national transport strategy, supervised by the cumbersome British Transport Commission (BTC). One trouble was that any profits the railways generated went into a single BTC kitty, where it could be siphoned off to fund works to canals, docks and harbours. To add to its troubles, the railways had to underwrite the compensation to railway shareholders resulting from nationalisation and amounting to an eye-watering £1,693,000,000. They also had to find £43 million to buy the private sector's fleet of 544,000 railway wagons – at a rate of compensation that by no means reflected their largely clapped-out state (55,000 of them had to be scrapped within a year of purchase). The railways also laboured under the Victorian burden of a common carrier requirement, under which they had to carry *any* cargo *anywhere*, however unprofitable, at a nationally agreed rate. Road hauliers were under no such obligation, which was not lifted until 1953.

As if things were not bad enough for the railways under Labour, they would get steadily worse from 1951 with a Conservative Government in place. The Conservatives did not like railways – they were nasty, communal, Socialist things. They scrapped Labour's national transport strategy and, under the Transport

Act 1953, put their own ideology in place. This was summarised in government memos of the time as:

> ... road haulage should be allowed to expand to the extent demanded by trade, industry and agriculture and the railways should effect such economies as they can to offset the resulting loss of traffic.

The rail industry thus found itself competing on an uneven playing field with a rejuvenated road haulage industry, on the basis that the railways had to pay for their own infrastructure, whilst road haulage got theirs funded by the government (albeit with a bit of help from road-fund licence payments). The Act also abolished central control of the railways, which would later lead to unnecessary local variation in equipment specifications for the railways and a failure to establish clear priorities for such investment as was available.

Notwithstanding all this, in December 1954 the Government published a comprehensive fifteen-year modernisation plan for the railways. This belatedly proposed the switch from steam to electric and diesel traction, and building vast new automated marshalling yards for the increase in freight traffic, which they (incorrectly) forecast would happen, new stations, rolling stock and signalling, not to mention the closure of some unprofitable lines. Whilst the Government was happy to take the political credit for the scheme, they would not put any money into it – the best British Railways could hope for was a government loan of part of the huge £1.2 billion cost (£22 billion at 2007 prices), repayable with interest.

Not only was the scheme unaffordable, it was poorly conceived. It tried to modernise the railways as they existed, without taking into account the changes taking place in demand. The new marshalling yards and the types of locomotive they specified were being built to serve a part of their business that was in free fall, particularly after the Government denationalised the road haulage industry.

To make things worse, the move to diesel and electric traction was poorly handled. One of the things the railways most needed was standardisation on a minimum number of proven models of locomotive. However, this was thwarted by a government that wanted a variety of models for British manufacturers to show off in the export market. The railways, therefore, found themselves saddled with a plethora of different models, none of which they were able to test thoroughly before their introduction and a number of which proved to be costly failures – some had to be withdrawn from service before the steam locomotives they were designed to replace.

By the time the plan came up for review in July 1959, it was clearly not going to achieve its objective of reversing British railways' losses by 1962. On the contrary, the industry's annual losses almost tripled (to £42 million) in the four years leading up to 1960. By then, the re-elected government had Ernest Marples, a man who had made his fortune from road building, as its Transport Minister. Thus the scene was set for Dr Beeching's railway cuts of the 1960s.

The Routemaster bus

In 1954, the first prototypes of a new bus made their appearance, the product of a joint initiative by London Transport and the manufacturer, AEC. They went through rigorous testing during production, and between 1958 and 1968 some 2,876 were built, virtually all of which were taken up by London Transport. The other main user was British European Airways, who had a model with a shorter wheelbase that could tow a trailer and was capable of 70mph. The Routemaster was to become an icon of Britain and, more particularly, of London.

The new Routemaster was a strange combination of cutting-edge technology and some ideas that, even when they first emerged, were criticised as being hopelessly obsolete. The original brief was that they should be lighter and easier to operate and maintain than the models they were to replace. They achieved this by using a lot of aluminium in the construction (which had the bonus of being corrosion-free), along with new construction techniques developed in wartime plane construction. It was undoubtedly very efficient; this sixty-four-seat model weighed in at ¾ ton less than the fifty-six-seat model it replaced and it offered greater fuel economy than even many more 'modern' (but lower-capacity) single-decker designs. It also featured new technology, such as an automatic gearbox, power steering and power-assisted hydraulic brakes.

At the same time, its front-engined, open rear access platform layout was considered completely out-of-date, at a time when informed opinion favoured a rear engine and front access, which also held out the possibility of one-person operation. Bus traditionalists also criticised the Routemaster's complexity and the fact that it pandered too much to the comfort of its passengers with its independent front suspension and heated passenger area. It was true to say that things like its automatic gearbox did initially prove unreliable; this may have been due in part to the fact that many of the first Routemasters were based in the depots of the trolley buses that they replaced, and that maintenance crews may have taken time to adapt from electric to modern diesel vehicles.

However, the fleet eventually became established and proved to be both popular and enduring – as late as 1994, almost all of London Transport's Routemaster fleet was being refurbished to give a further ten years' service. By then, deregulation of bus services had taken place, and this gave rise to a new surge of interest in the Routemaster. Established bus operators around the country bought them up as a means of expanding their fleets quickly to crowd out any competition, and newcomers to bus operation saw them as a cheap way of entering the market. Re-engined and refurbished, Routemasters survived to outlive many of the models that were designed to replace them.

In 2001, London Mayor Ken Livingstone was quoted as saying that 'only some kind of ghastly dehumanised moron would want to get rid of the Routemasters'. Predictably, in 2003 it was announced that London's Routemasters were to be phased out. A number of factors were starting to tell against them. There were the inevitable additional costs arising from two-man, as opposed to one-man, operation. The advantage of faster boarding that two-man operation gave began to be eroded by the growth in off-bus ticket sales, Oyster cards, and so on. There was a safety issue associated with the open platform access, and varying statistics reported that anything between three and ten people a year were being killed in accidents relating to boarding or disembarking from Routemasters. More fundamentally, it was impossible to make Routemasters wheelchair accessible, something that becomes a statutory requirement for buses from 2017. London's last scheduled Routemaster services (apart from two heritage services) were gone by 2005. However, they can still be seen on private hire, doing promotional work or serving as tourist attractions in their own right, both in Britain and across the world. The single-decker, bendy buses that replaced them are themselves very swiftly being phased out and replaced by what is described as a new Routemaster design for the twenty-first century.

The Things They Say About the 1950s

Quotations about the decade itself, the people in public life at the time and other events of the decade.

The decade

Jonathan Miller (1999) 'England was stuck in the Thirties until the Sixties.'

Eric Hobsbawm (2002) 'The fifties are the crucial decade. For the first time you could feel things changing. Suez and the coming of rock and roll divide twentieth-century British history.'

Harold Macmillan (1957) 'Let's be frank about it; most of our people have never had it so good. Go around the country, go to the industrial towns, go to the farms and you will see a state of prosperity such as we have never had in our lifetime – nor indeed ever in the history of this country. What is beginning to worry some of us is "is it too good to be true?" or perhaps I should say "is it too good to last?"'

(Macmillan's famous 'never had it so good' speech was in fact a dire warning about the perils of inflation. In fact, 'never had it so good' was originally a slogan coined by the American Democrats in 1952.)

Peter Lewis (1978) 'No period that paid extravagant attention to both Marilyn Monroe and John Foster Dulles, to Billy Graham and James Dean, can be called simple or consistent. It was a time when life was real, life was earnest, for most people (it normally is). But it was a time when hope outweighed despair or cynicism. It was a time when it was pleasant to be young enough to feel concerned, mildly rebellious and naively optimistic that solutions could be found.'

(From the preface to his book *The 50s*.)

Blake Morrison (2005) '[The fifties] seem magically cosy and placid – like a becalmed liner, adrift from the dramas on the mainland ... Few could feel nostalgic for the jingoism, class division, snobbery, racism, insularity, complacency, bureaucratic meddling and all-pervasive political incorrectness of the period. But in the provinces at least, Britain seemed a safer place then, freer, friendlier, more trusting. And despite the narrow-mindedness, it could also be strangely tolerant.'

(From his foreword to Ken Blakemore's book, *Sunnyside Down: Growing up in 1950s Britain*.)

Politics: Harmony within the 1950s Conservative government

Butler on Eden: 'Half mad baronet, half beautiful woman.'

(A reference to Eden's parents. When asked whether he supported Eden, Butler said, 'He is the best Prime Minister we have.')

Eden on Butler: 'I wish Butler were a man I could respect ... LG [David Lloyd George] once called him "the artful dodger" but if this is important in politics, it is also not enough.'

Macmillan on Eden: 'Very excitable, very feminine-type, very easily upset, easily annoyed.'

(He also said that 'the trouble with Anthony Eden was that he was trained to win the Derby in 1938; unfortunately he was not let out of the starting stalls until 1955', and that Eden was 'forever poised between a cliché and an indiscretion.')

Eden on Macmillan: 'A vulgarian and at heart untrustworthy.'

Winston Churchill on Clement Attlee (1954): 'Clement Attlee is a modest man who has a good deal to be modest about.'

(Churchill also referred to Attlee as 'a sheep in sheep's clothing'. Attlee was nearly killed at the disastrous Gallipoli campaign in the First World War, for which Churchill was in no small part responsible.)

Clement Attlee on Winston Churchill: 'A monologue is not a decision.'

(When Churchill complained that a matter had been raised several times in Cabinet. He also said that Churchill was fifty per cent genius, fifty per cent bloody fool.)

Aneurin Bevan on Clement Attlee: 'He brings to the fierce struggle of politics the tepid enthusiasm of a lazy summer afternoon at a cricket match.'

Harold Macmillan (1951): 'A strange monastic-looking man, emaciated and said to live off watercress grown off the blotting paper on his desk.'

(Speaking of the austerely vegetarian Socialist politician Sir Stafford Cripps)

The 1950s media

Winston Churchill (*circa* 1954): 'I am no enthusiast for the television age, in which I fear mass thought and actions will be taken charge of by machinery, both destructive and distracting.'

BBC report on early audience responses to *The Goon Show* (1951): 'One section of the audience found this an amusing and original show, but there are apparently many still listening to it for whom the "crazy" type of humour and accompanying "noisiness" have no attraction.'

Peter Eton (a producer of *The Goon Show*): 'We were trying to undermine the standing order. We were anti-Commonwealth, anti-Empire, anti-bureaucrat, anti-armed forces.'

BBC Working Party report (1957): 'There [has] been a profound change of mood in the country, particularly among its younger members, which [makes] the paternalistic flavour of the 1945 [BBC] policy less acceptable ... Entertainment should not be undervalued.'

Roy Thompson: 'A licence to print money.'

(How he famously described holding a commercial television broadcasting franchise in the late 1950s.)

Captain Tom Brownrigg of Associated–Rediffusion (1958): 'I see no reason why we should pour out money just to be better than the BBC at something which ought, in any case, be the BBC's prime responsibility!'

(Commercial television sets out its populist stall.)

Bernard Levin (1956): 'What does Sir Robert think he has proven if he shows that more people watch ITA than the BBC? Does he know how many people watched the last public execution to take place in this country?'

(For balance, the *Guardian* sets out the anti-populist stall.)

Anthony Eden criticising BBC coverage of the Suez crisis (1956): 'The BBC is exasperating me by leaning over backwards to be what they call neutral and to present both sides of the case.'

He also lied to Parliament about the affair, saying:

'I want to say this on the question of foreknowledge, and to say it quite bluntly to the House, that there was not foreknowledge that Israel would attack Egypt – there was not.'

Anthony Eden also said of Suez:

'We are not at war with Egypt. We are in an armed conflict.'

1950s food

Good Living: 'Good food and plenty of it, full employment, well-furnished homes – today's generation knows what Good Living really means!'

(From an advertisement for New Zealand butter in 1957.)

German political theorist Hannah Arendt when visiting Manchester in 1952: 'A dull blanket of fear lies over the country, which is softened, though, by the fact that they've been eating too little for such a long time that they barely notice the difference any more. And yet it's almost unbelievable. Not just what the shops look like – groceries and so on, everything scarce, everything of bad quality ... but also their genius to make life uncomfortable. Everything set up as if expressively to make life difficult, or at least to challenge you to muster so much cheerfulness that everything can be overcome.'

Elizabeth David from her *French Country Cooking* (1951): 'Rationing, the disappearance of servants, and the bad and expensive meals served in restaurants, have led English women to take a far greater interest in food than was formerly considered polite.'

Assorted quotes

Lionel Brett talking about the Festival of Britain in the *Observer* (1951): 'The great thing is that, in a single stride, though working under every possible handicap, our designers have unmistakeably taken the lead ... They have put on a show so impossible not to enjoy that there is a real hope that it will mark the beginning of a modern style which will be generally accepted.'

Cecil Beaton on men's fashions (1955): 'Young "teddy boys" with their bright blue or scarlet corduroy pants, seem to show spirit, but generally men go about in dirty old mackintoshes, shiny striped City trousers, and greasy bowlers. The English have not recovered from the war, and it shows itself in the torpor of their vestments.'

Reginald Maudling (1951): 'The difficulty today is not to find jobs for people, but people for jobs.'

Peter Wildeblood on his homosexuality, for which he was imprisoned in a famous case in 1954: 'I am no more proud of my condition than I would be of having a glass eye or a hare-lip. On the other hand, I am no more ashamed of it than I would be of being colour-blind or of writing with my left hand.'

And finally …

Me, from the introduction to my book *From Rationing to Rock* (1998): 'They used to say that, if you could remember the swinging sixties, you weren't in them. The fifties are different – if you can remember them, you are doing awfully well for your age.'

Tragedies

Sadly, the 1950s were no more exempt than any other decade to their share of natural and manmade disasters. We remember some of them here.

The Cardiff Air Disaster 1950

In March 1950, a group of Welsh rugby supporters decided to go to Dublin and support the national side in their bid to win the Triple Crown for the first time since 1911. They had originally planned to charter two planes but the charter company, Fairflight, said they could fit them all into one, by stripping out the plane and fitting extra seats.

The aircraft they were using was the Avro Tudor, a civilian derivative of the Mark VI wartime Lancaster bomber. The aircraft did not have an unblemished safety record. BOAC had refused to use it as a passenger aircraft, and twice in the previous two years versions of it had been grounded, following fatal accidents. Its designer, Roy Chadwick, had himself been killed in one, although this was nothing to do with the aircraft's design – during routine servicing two of its aileron control wires had been accidentally crossed, with the result that pulling the stick to go up made you go down. The charter aircraft itself had seen hard service as a fuel tanker during the Berlin airlift.

The flight to Dublin was uneventful and the match went to Wales, so the seventy-eight passengers were in high spirits on the return journey as the plane came into land at Llandow airport, near Cardiff. Eyewitnesses said the plane came in too low, and the pilot tried to correct this by opening the throttles; the plane climbed steeply, then stalled and fell, breaking into pieces as it hit the ground. Seventy-five of the passengers and all five crew were killed, in what was then (and would remain for some years) the world's worst air disaster.

The charter company tried to pin the accident on pilot error, but the Committee of Enquiry dismissed this as 'inherently improbable'. They decided that by fitting the extra seats, the charter company had fundamentally shifted the plane's centre of gravity, reducing the effectiveness of the elevators. They were found guilty of contravening the plane's certificate of airworthiness and were fined £50 (which works out at roughly 62p per person killed) plus £100 costs. The following year, the company became part of the Freddie Laker aviation empire.

Lynmouth floods 1952

August 1952 was a very damp month from the outset, with above average rainfall. By the middle of the month, the ground on Exmoor, above the little Devon seaside resort of Lynmouth, was already saturated, and the rocks that underlay it were impermeable, so any further rainfall had nowhere to go. On the night of 15th August, the area was hit by a freak storm, in which 9in of rain fell in just twenty-four hours. The water rapidly found its way into the rivers East and West Lyn, which converged in the steep valley leading down into Lynmouth. An estimated 90 million tonnes of water swept down into the town, in a torrent so fierce that it carried boulders and trees with it. During the clear up afterwards, some 144,000 tonnes of debris had to be removed from the town.

The river channels could not contain the waters, which swept through the streets, destroying a hundred buildings and twenty-eight of the town's thirty-one bridges. In total, thirty-eight cars were washed out to sea and 420 people were left homeless. Thirty-four people died. One eyewitness spoke of a row of cottages being 'folded up like a pack of cards' and said that the screams of those trapped inside could be heard above the roaring of the waters. In the midst of the chaos, there were acts of heroism – local police officer Derek Harper received the George Medal for his attempts to rescue people, and thirteen others received gallantry awards.

The cost of the damage was estimated to be between £3–5 million (at 1952 prices) and an Emergency Relief fund rapidly raised donations of £500,000. All the basic services had been knocked out, and the town had to be totally evacuated whilst it was substantially rebuilt after the floods. The river was realigned and made better able to cope with a similar event in future – new bridges were reinforced and so designed that they would not be blocked by debris.

Lynmouth had suffered flooding events before – in 1607 and 1796 – but the severity of this one, with 250 times the normal August rainfall, had some people looking for sinister explanations. One conspiracy theory centred round an allegation that the Ministry of Defence had been conducting experiments in 'cloud seeding' just before the disaster. This involved dropping chemicals (dry ice, salt and silver iodide have been suggested as possibilities) into clouds to bring on exceptionally heavy rain, as a means of bogging down an enemy. The conspiracy theorists felt vindicated by the fact that classified official documents relating to the experiment had conveniently 'gone missing', but positive proof has so far been harder to come by.

Harrow rail disaster 1952

The morning of 8 October 1952 started out like any other commuting day. In Harrow and Wealdstone station, on the northern tip of London, the 7.31 local passenger service from Tring was picking up passengers on the fast platform, ready to run at high speed into its destination, London Euston. Just as it was about to leave, it was struck in the rear by the overnight sleeper from Perth, running an hour late and travelling at between 50–60mph. Within seconds, the express service to Manchester and Liverpool, travelling on the down fast line, ploughed into the strewn wreckage at about 50mph. The coaches slewed across the platforms, sweeping commuters before them, and reared up to a height of some 30ft, taking out part of a pedestrian bridge. All six tracks were now blocked and Harrow had just made its name as home to England's worst (and Britain's worst peacetime) rail accident. It was estimated that over a thousand people had been travelling in the three trains, with many more waiting on the platforms. In total, 112 people were killed and some 340 injured.

The cause of the accident was a mystery, one that was not helped by the fact that the key witnesses – the driver and the fireman of the Perth train – were both killed in the accident. It was said that the driver of the Perth train (an experienced driver, regarded by his colleagues as 'cautious') went through one signal at caution and two at red. There was a bit of fog around that morning, though conditions were improving, and the possibility was raised that smoke or steam from another train had temporarily obscured the signals. In any event, these would only have been visible for about four seconds at the speed the train was travelling. A post-mortem examination on the Perth train driver revealed no sudden health failure that might have caused him to miss the signals and the enquiry into the accident laid the blame at his door. No blame was ever attached to the local signalling staff and the signals were found to be in perfect working order. The driver of the Manchester/Liverpool train was held to be the victim of someone else's crash, whose debris he could not have avoided. His train, like the one from Perth, had been running late. Had it been on time, it would have avoided the carnage.

Emergency teams worked feverishly all day and into the following night to free passengers trapped in the mountain of twisted metal that engulfed the station, but they were overwhelmed by the sheer scale of the tragedy, and their rescue attempts were uncoordinated and lacking in overall leadership.

They were joined by rescuers from a nearby United States Air Force base, who arranged for supplies of blood and painkillers to be flown in from one of their bases in Lancashire, and who set up a field hospital on platforms 5 and 6. The NHS and the emergency services learned much that day, from the way in which the Americans applied battlefield medical techniques to a civilian disaster. For their part, British Railways announced (with some understatement) that there would have to be changes to the timetables into and out of Euston, and that local postal services might be disrupted.

Unsurprisingly, there were calls for improved safety systems on trains, such as the former Great Western Railway's Automatic Warning System, which they had been using successfully since 1905. Efforts had been made for years to standardise it across the railway network, but these had been resisted on cost grounds, and technical arguments about whether it would work in other parts of the country. The Harrow disaster marked an effective end to that resistance.

Air display disaster 1952

One of the highlights of the 1952 Farnborough Air Show was set to be a demonstration of the De Havilland 110, the new supersonic jet fighter being developed for the Royal Navy. It was a visually striking aeroplane with a twin boom tail, and was being flown by John Derry. He was something of a national hero, having become the first Briton to break the sound barrier in 1948.

On the morning of 6 September, the regular demonstration aircraft was out of action with engine problems and a spare had to be collected hurriedly from the factory. The first part of the demonstration went to plan, with Derry impressively breaking the sound barrier and performing a low pass in front of the crowd, but as he climbed out of the low pass, first the outer part of the starboard wing, then the outer port wing, followed by the engines and cockpit, fell off the plane. This naturally affected its handling. More seriously, parts of the aircraft fell into the crowd and twenty-nine spectators were killed, along with Derry and an observer who was travelling with him in the aircraft. The failure was later attributed to a faulty wing design, which had been largely copied from an earlier, slower and lighter aircraft, the DH Vampire.

Amazingly, within an hour, and after the debris had been cleared up, the show was allowed to continue, with Derry's friend and fellow test pilot, Neville Duke, performing a similar supersonic display in his new Hawker Hunter. Two main consequences flowed from this tragedy. First, the design of the DH110 was modified and it would enter into service in 1959 as the Sea Vixen, where it operated satisfactorily into the 1970s. Second, the rules governing air shows were tightened up. In future, displays involving jets had to keep 750ft away from the crowd in straight flight and 1,480ft away if any manoeuvring was taking place.

Car ferry sinking 1953

The end of January 1953 saw much of England and beyond subjected to some of the worst weather of the century. The weather forecasts said it would be bad, but even they did not anticipate force-twelve gales with 100mph winds, whipping up 50ft waves in the Irish Sea. It was into these conditions that the British Railways car ferry, the *Princess Victoria*, set out on the short crossing between Stranraer and Larne in Northern Ireland. She was a relatively modern vessel, launched in 1947, and the first roll-on roll-off car ferry to operate in British waters.

An hour out from Stranraer, Captain James Ferguson realised that he was in some difficulty. It is thought he may have tried to turn around and head back into the harbour, but this would just have exposed his vulnerable rear car doors to the full fury of the storm. The boat had additional protection for this part of the vessel in the form of spray doors, but they took so long to raise and lower that they were rarely used. The car deck started to take in water, which caused the boat to list. This exposed a second design flaw in the vessel – the scuppers, through which any such water was supposed to be drained, did not work properly, allowing the water to accumulate. The listing caused cargo to break loose from its fixings and slide down the now sloping decks, making the listing worse. By the time the Captain gave the order to abandon ship, the vessel was keeling over so badly that it was nigh impossible to launch the lifeboats.

From the moment the captain started sending calls for help, a rescue mission began, but it proved to be one failure after another. First, the *Princess Victoria* could only communicate in Morse code, whereas those that she needed to communicate with used radio, leading to delays. Second, the terminology used by the captain led to confusion. He spoke of the vessel being 'not under command', which others took to mean she was engineless and drifting. They made assumptions about her location on that basis, whereas she was in fact still under power and now heading towards Ireland, having abandoned any attempt to return to Stranraer. Naval ships and aircraft were both, for various reasons, delayed in going out to look for her. Appalling visibility did not help the search when it did get under way. Even when would-be rescuers arrived on the scene, the mountainous waves made it almost impossible to get people on board the vessel. Around 130 passengers and crew perished in the wreck, and just forty-four survivors were recovered.

In a conspicuous act of gallantry for which he received a posthumous George Medal, the ship's radio officer, David Broadfoot, stayed at his post, transmitting messages until the ship went down, and Captain Ferguson was last seen standing at a salute in the bridge of his stricken vessel, in the finest naval tradition.

The Committee of Inquiry correctly identified the design faults in the vessel as a contributory factor in the disaster, and lessons were learned for the design of future roll-on roll-off ferries.

February floods 1953

The same freak weather had disastrous consequences along the length of the east coast, from Scotland to the English Channel, and over into Netherlands and Belgium. A combination of a high spring tide, strong winds and high atmospheric pressure created a storm tide, in which the waters rose to 18ft 4in above mean sea level, overwhelming defences the length of the coast. No adequate warnings were given, since techniques for forecasting such events were primitive at the time, and there was no one agency responsible for issuing warnings. Added to this, the event occurred on a Saturday night, when radio stations had ceased to broadcast and some smaller weather stations did not operate on a twenty-four-hour basis. In any event, the onset of the flooding could be terrifyingly swift. In Harwich, eyewitnesses saw a 2m-high rolling wall of water sweep down Albert Street.

A few statistics may help to illustrate the scale of the disaster:

> 160,000 acres of land was inundated by the sea (some of it two miles inland)
> 30,000 people had to be evacuated
> 24,000 properties were seriously damaged
> £5 billion worth of damage (in today's money)
> 46,000 head of livestock were lost
> 307 people died

It was described as Britain's greatest natural disaster of the century. About 70 per cent of the deaths were concentrated to a small number of communities – such as Mablethorpe and Snettisham (sixty-five dead), Felixstowe and Harwich (over forty), Jaywick, near Clacton (thirty-seven, representing 5 per cent of the village's population), and Canvey Island (fifty-eight). In many cases, the victims were living in insubstantial single-storey wooden houses, some of which were built pre-war as holiday homes and were not even intended as year-round accommodation – such was the post-war housing shortage. Many of these properties were simply picked up by the water and swept along for hundreds of metres. Even those in more substantial brick-built houses found themselves at risk from trees and other debris that was being swept along in the flood and could punch holes in their walls.

Among the casualties were the elderly and disabled, who would have found it harder to get away from the rushing waters. Many of their more mobile neighbours were able to climb onto their rooves and cling on, in hope of rescue. For some, rescue did not come in time. Exhausted and freezing in the arctic storm that was blowing around them, they either died of hypothermia or fell to their deaths in the water below – about a third of the deaths were down to factors other than drowning, such as hypothermia.

The following day, rescue efforts swung into action. A Dunkirk-style flotilla of small boats went to rescue the inhabitants of the island of Fowlness, off the coast of Essex. United States Air Force personnel were among the first to mount a rescue initiative. Soon, all those affected by the flooding were receiving help of one kind or another and some 30,000 people – many of them British or American military personnel – were at work, repairing the flood defences. The whole of Canvey Island had been under water – in places to a depth of 2–3m. All of its essential services were down, and a decision was made on the Sunday morning to evacuate all 12,000 inhabitants of the island. In the longer term, it is thought that exposure to the flooding led to an increase in death from respiratory diseases. The fact that these events occurred in the middle of a national influenza epidemic cannot have helped.

A committee was set up under the chairmanship of Viscount Waverley to learn the lessons of the disaster, and their report was to form the basis for government policy on coastal flooding for the rest of the century. Canvey Island was enclosed by higher sea walls, and its population is now double what it was in 1953. Sea defences were strengthened elsewhere. Kings Lynn, for example, also raised its sea walls; just as well because in January 1978 they experienced a storm surge even greater than that of 1953. A combination of improved defences and luck (in that the winds were not as strong) meant that the 1978 floods were much less serious. London only narrowly avoided being flooded in 1953 and the committee made recommendations about protecting the capital. However, it took until 1982 for the Thames Barrage to become a reality.

Could this disaster have been foreseen, and how likely is it to happen again? The coast had only recently (in 1949) suffered what was then described as its worst flooding in sixty-five years, and this should have at least forewarned the authorities about the parlous state of our coastal defences, neglected as they had been during the war years. As for it happening again, it was calculated in 1953 that the combination of factors that produced the water levels of the great flood was a one in two-hundred year event. However, by the middle of this century, with global warming a factor, the odds are forecast to shorten to one in one-hundred years.

Sutton Coldfield rail disaster 1955

It was a Sunday afternoon in January 1955. The York to Bristol express was approaching the station at Sutton Coldfield, just outside Birmingham, carrying about 300 passengers. Weekend engineering works meant that it had been diverted from its usual route and the regular driver did not know the new line. As railway regulations required, he was given a 'conductor' driver, who knew the route. The rule was that the two of them should jointly drive the train but the regular driver, who was finding the rough riding of the locomotive tiring, decided after a while to leave it to the conductor, while he retired to the front carriage.

The train approached Sutton Coldfield station at 55–60 mph, but this stretch of track was subject to a 30mph speed limit. As it entered the station, the driver found out why; the locomotive left the track, causing nine of its ten coaches to topple over, crashing into the station platforms and buildings. Seventeen people were killed (and, depending on which account you believe, anything between 23 and 43 people were injured). An even bigger disaster was only avoided by the quick thinking of some off-duty railwaymen who had been travelling on the train. They were able to get out and run to the nearby signal box to alert staff, before any other train reached the crash site.

It was no difficulty for the Committee of Inquiry to establish that the cause of the crash was excess speed, but why was the conductor driver going so fast on a stretch of line that he was supposed to know? Both he and the fireman were killed in the crash, so the matter had to be the subject of speculation. It was variously suggested:

✳ that he was trying to make up time, because the train was running late

✳ that he was increasing speed to tackle the gradient that came immediately after the station

✳ that the train had no speedometer, which was quite common at that time

✳ that the rough riding of the locomotive, which had fatigued the regular driver, had caused him to misjudge the speed. It was also the case that the locomotive was rather more powerful than the ones the conductor driver was accustomed to

The regular driver was badly injured in the crash, but survived. He was criticised for leaving the cab. Even if he did not know the route, he was still formally responsible for the safety of the train and its passengers. The one other shortcoming the committee could point to was the lack of reminder signs about the speed restriction. Today, any driver exceeding the speed limit automatically gets an audible warning in his cab; a similar accident, therefore, should not happen.

Lewisham rail disaster 1957

The homeward commute, on a December evening in 1957, was a miserable affair. The usual crush of working people was supplemented by crowds of Christmas shoppers, and an estimated 1,500 people were packed into the 5.18 from Charing Cross to Hayes. To add to the misery, one of London's smogs had descended, reducing visibility to 20 yards in places. Their train was held at a signal just outside St John's Station, while the signalman peered through the murk to try to establish their destination.

Suddenly the train suffered a terrific blow from behind. The steam-hauled service from Cannon Street to Ramsgate, travelling at about 35mph, had gone into the back of it. The rear carriages of the commuter train were telescoped together and the steam train, its tender and some of its carriages were thrown off the tracks. The tender demolished some of the columns holding up the Nunhead flyover, which promptly collapsed onto the carriages, squashing them flat. A third train was just about to go over the viaduct, but the driver managed to stop it on the very brink of dropping onto the accident scene and reverse it to safety.

Rescue workers were soon on the scene, but it was difficult and dangerous working among the tangled remains of railway coaches and the flyover, which had to be cut into 10-ton pieces and removed from the accident scene. Around ninety people were killed and 176 injured in the crash, and local emergency services were soon overwhelmed. There were so many fatalities on stretchers that they did not have enough to transport the living. Injured passengers had to be ferried down a steep bank and over a high wall to reach the waiting ambulances.

What was clear to the Committee of Inquiry was that the driver of the steam train had missed two signals in the difficult, foggy conditions, and the majority of the blame for the accident was laid at his door. He was tried for manslaughter, but the case could not be brought to a conclusion when it became clear that the trauma of it had severely impaired his mental state. In addition, there were extenuating circumstances. The signals on this stretch of track were placed on the right-hand side, whereas most steam trains were left-hand drive, making it very difficult for the driver to see them round the steam locomotive's boiler. Normally, the driver would have the fireman (or stoker) look out to the right for him, but for some reason this had not happened in this case. British Railways were also held to have some responsibility, because of their slow rate of progress in fitting the Automatic Warning System, which would have prevented an accident like this (despite the warning sounded after the Harrow disaster). AWS only became mandatory forty years later, in 1997.

Crazy Cats – Teenage Music of the 1950s

'Rock and roll is mainly performed by coloured artists for coloured people and is therefore unlikely ever to prove popular in Britain.'

(Ted Heath, British dance band leader, 25 May 1956)

*I*n this chapter we look at the musical tastes of the 1950s teenager. Their dress sense is dealt with in the chapter on fashion.

Johnnie Ray - The Prince of Wails

It is sometimes thought that Elvis Presley and rock and roll burst onto an unsuspecting world without warning, but Johnnie Ray provided a transition between Elvis and the earlier generation of crooners led by Frank Sinatra. Johnnie Ray was born in Oregon in 1927 and showed early talent as a keyboard player. At the age of thirteen, he suffered an accident that left him deaf in one ear – something left untreated for some years, and which would have a marked impact upon his future career.

By the start of the 1950s, he was developing an act that combined conventional pop music with R&B (he was often mistaken by those who had not seen him perform for a black female singer). He had a minor hit, in 1951, with a self-penned song called 'Whiskey and Gin', but it was the following year that he released the double A-side that launched him into stardom – 'Cry' and 'The Little White Cloud that Cried'. By March 1952, he occupied three of the top places in the American charts and enjoyed twenty-five American Top Thirty hits between 1952 and 1957.

By now, he had established his own extraordinary stage persona. Perspiring profusely (previously, vocalists were not allowed to admit to the possession of sweat glands) and weeping uncontrollably, he would tear at his hair, throw himself about the stage and seduce the microphone. His voice would ascend into a choking, whining upper register and his words were hopelessly elongated in their enunciation. It was, as one reviewer put it, 'either moving or pathetic, depending on your stand'. The critics labelled him the 'Nabob of Sob', the 'Prince of Wails' and the 'Cry Guy'. Regardless, plenty of young women found it moving enough to want to mob him and tear bits off his clothing.

There are two theories as to why his deafness might have contributed to this unique delivery. One was that the isolation caused by his long-undiagnosed partial deafness (which became almost complete after surgery on his ears in 1958 went wrong) created an angst that came out in his performances. The other was that the large, primitive hearing aids of the day, which became a hallmark of his performances, were ill suited to stage performances and had an effect on his delivery.

In his day, he was hugely influential – both Bob Dylan and Elvis Presley considered themselves devotees, and when Presley was originally launched, he was billed as 'the most important singing find since Johnnie Ray.' More curiously, Morrissey of The Smiths used to wear a hearing aid on stage as homage to Ray – despite the fact that he had nothing wrong with his hearing. One person who could not stand Ray (to the point where he once punched him) was Frank Sinatra – perhaps because his then wife, Ava Gardner, was said to have been fascinated with him.

Despite having an adoring female following and a (short-lived) marriage, Ray's bisexuality caused a dent in his popularity, particularly when he tried to seduce an undercover police officer (this being illegal at the time). His other problem was with alcoholism – he would be diagnosed with cirrhosis at the age of fifty and die of liver failure in 1990, aged sixty-three. As his popularity in America went into decline, he turned to his overseas admirers. They – in particular, those in the United Kingdom – proved much more durable. On his first visit to England, he was able to fill the London Palladium for three straight weeks and his performance twenty years later earned him a fifteen-minute standing ovation.

Some modern audiences may find Ray's attraction a little hard to understand today. Ray himself was asked to explain it. He said that his only real claim to fame was that: 'I am an original ... I've got no talent. Still sing flat as a table. I'm a sort of human spaniel. People come to see what I'm like. I make them feel, I exhaust them, I destroy them.'

Bill Haley and His Comets – Rock Around the Clock

Rock and roll may owe its origins to a yodelling cowboy from Detroit. In the 1940s, Bill Haley's reputation was as a top yodeller, and he would not be seen on stage without a Stetson and all of his western attire. He sang with the Down Homers, the Range Drifters, the Four Aces of Western Swing and – the group that would find fame under another name – Bill Haley and his Saddlemen. Haley liked to experiment with different sounds and he picked up the idea from rockabilly of a slap-back bass, to give a more percussive sound to the music. One thing cowboy bands definitely did not have at this time was any percussion in the form of drums but, like a number of musicians, Haley was working towards a fusion of country music and rhythm and blues. A drummer duly arrived in 1953.

As their music got increasingly hard-edged, the band's name and their fancy dress became increasingly incongruous. Someone mixed up the names Haley and Halley – the latter the discoverer of the comet that took his name – and suggested they became Bill Haley and His Comets. The group's first modest success was with a number called 'Crazy Man, Crazy', which was used as the soundtrack to a television play starring James Dean in 1953. The band signed a new recording contract with Decca in April 1954 and later that same month they recorded 'Rock Around the Clock'. It was released (as a B-side) in May, but at first enjoyed only limited success. It only really took off in 1955, when it was used as the soundtrack to the film *Blackboard Jungle*.

Although it may be the song the band will forever be associated with, 'Rock Around the Clock' was not their first hit. 'Shake Rattle and Roll' had already reached number four in the American charts in December 1954. This was a cleaned-up version of a Big Joe Turner song. ('Get out of that bed and wash your face and hands' became 'get out of that kitchen and rattle those pots and pans' to protect delicate sensibilities). 'Rock Around the Clock' was also a hit in Britain several months before it broke through in America, reaching number seventeen in our charts in January 1955. Between late 1954 and late 1956, the band had nine singles in the charts, including a number one and three more in the top ten.

By now, the band had traded their cowboy outfits for matching dinner suits in a lurid Rupert Bear check, and they livened up their act with acrobatic antics by their double bass and saxophone players. The chubby, elderly (in rock and roll terms) Haley, with his kiss curl, was not the stuff of which rock idols were made. (One explanation for the curl was that Haley was self-conscious about his left eye, which had been blind from childhood, and had cultivated it over his other eye to draw attention away from it.) Haley's popularity in America began to wane from 1956–7, as younger, sexier products such as Elvis and Jerry Lee Lewis came on the market. The band then started to trade on their popularity overseas where they found more enduring fame; something that became rather more essential in later years because of Haley's tax problems in the United States. Haley's last performance in Britain was in November 1979, in front of the Queen, just two years before his death in 1981.

The time had come for rock and roll. Whilst Haley and others were moving towards it from a country music direction, others, like Chuck Berry, Bo Diddley and Little Richard, were getting there from a starting point in rhythm and blues. But why 'rock and roll'? Haley claimed to have invented the term whilst writing a song lyric, but it has a much longer history. There was a modern usage going back to 1934. Before that, Shakespeare used the term 'rock' to mean to shake up, disturb or incite, and the word 'roll' has long been a euphemism for sexual intercourse. The two terms had even been brought together in the traditional sea shanty 'One More Day':

'Oh do, me Johnny Bowker
Come rock and roll me over'

'Rock Around the Clock' and its associations with the film industry (*Blackboard Jungle* was followed by the film of

Rock Around the Clock) became a by-word for youthful disorder, with hooligans wrecking the cinemas at which it was shown and laying waste to the surrounding area as they left the premises. Early showings at some 300 cinemas passed without problems, but it is thought that word reached Britain of rock and roll riots at American showings of the film, inspiring hooligans at home. Dancing in the aisles escalated into the throwing of lighted cigarettes and (unlit) light bulbs, seat slashing and the discharge of fire hoses. Outside, the jiving spread into the streets and onto the bonnets of parked cars. Bishops warned of the maddening effects of these hypnotic rhythms on young people and magistrates lamented their powerlessness to administer a damned good thrashing to the perpetrators.

Similar problems occurred when Haley and the Comets came to London in February 1957. Rioting fans at a railway station caused what the press christened 'the second battle of Waterloo'. Music critics who attended some of the early concerts found themselves lacking the vocabulary to describe their blend of wild music, pelvis wiggling (Haley was at it before Elvis perfected it) and amateur gymnastics on a double bass, and had to fall back on unlikely classical analogies with Beethoven and Carl Orff. Equally bewildered by the genre were the record company themselves, who initially described 'Rock Around the Clock' as a 'novelty foxtrot'.

Inevitably, this American craze gave rise in Britain to home-grown imitations. Who can forget Thomas Hicks, Harold Webb and Ronald Wycherley? (Most of us, probably, unless reminded that they changed their names to Tommy Steele, Cliff Richard and Billy Fury.) The idea that one needed talent to get into the musical limelight began to break down, as the use of the disc jockey at previously live venues got under way.

'Rock Around the Clock' is often seen as the official start of the rock and roll era, but there are plenty of earlier records that could lay claim to the title. They include:

'Good Rockin' Tonight' – Wynonie Harris (1948)

'Rock the Joint' – Jimmy Preston (1949)

'Rolling' and Tumblin'' – Muddy Waters (1950)

'Rocket 88' – Jackie Brenston (1951)

Elvis Presley

For a man who would come to be known as 'the King', Elvis Presley was born in very humble circumstances, in a two-room shack in Tupelo, Mississippi, in 1935. First, that name – it was his own, his parents being Vernon Elvis and Gladys Love Presley. He was an only child and had an impoverished upbringing, even more so after his father was imprisoned for cheque forgery in 1938 and the family were made homeless.

He was given a cheap guitar for his tenth birthday – apparently, he had been hoping for a bicycle or a rifle – but his early attempts at music making were not universally appreciated. His school music teacher told him he had no aptitude for singing, and he was turned down in auditions for a local singing group, the Songfellows (who told him he couldn't sing) and as vocalist for a local band (who told him to stick to his job as a truck driver). In 1953, he paid for some studio time at the local Sun recording studio (he later claimed it was to cut a disc as a present for his mother) and he caught the attention of the proprietor, Sam Phillips. However, when Phillips later arranged a trial studio session with Elvis, guitarist 'Scotty' Moore and bass player Bill Black, they failed to gel until very late in the session when Elvis started improvising with the song 'That's All Right, Mama'. The others joined in and they had found their sound. Elvis became a leading exponent of rockabilly, a fusion of country music and rhythm and blues, and the rest is history.

Elvis recorded five singles for Sun, before signing up with RCA in a deal brokered by the man who would become his manager for twenty years, Colonel Tom Parker. His first RCA recording, 'Heartbreak Hotel', was released in January 1956 and he made his film debut in November of that year with *Love Me Tender*. His stage persona caused some nervousness with conservative elements in television, and his energetic hip shaking earned him the nickname 'Elvis the Pelvis' – it was deemed too erotic for impressionable viewers, and he could only be shown on television from the waist up (it seems this mannerism came from a combination of a strong response to the rhythm of the music and sheer stage fright).

Conscription into the army in 1958 brought his career to a temporary halt, but it was resumed two years later. At first, he concentrated on films and soundtrack albums, doing few live concerts, but the films got steadily more formulaic, the music more mediocre and the sales correspondingly smaller. By 1968, many in the industry were writing him off as a has-been. Then, after a seven-year gap in live performances, he starred in a television Christmas special that rejuvenated his career, leading to an extended cabaret season at Las Vegas and profitable concert tours. In 1973, his Aloha From Hawaii concert was broadcast worldwide by satellite and was seen by 1.5 billion people. Unfortunately, his fondness for prescription drugs contributed to his death in 1977, at the age of just forty-two.

Elvis never performed in England, so the nearest his fans here got to him were his film and television performances. For a long time, it was thought that he only ever set foot in Britain for a two-hour stopover at Prestwick Airport, in March 1960. However, it later emerged that he had a secret one-day visit to London in 1958, in which he was given a conducted tour of the city by one of Britain's own rock and roll stars, Tommy Steele.

Skiffle

'Skiffle' was one of the names the impoverished black residents of 1920s and 1930s Chicago gave to their improvised music. They would pick up anything that would make a noise – comb and paper, washboard, a jug, as well as the more conventional guitars and banjos – to generate music that (they hoped) would also generate money to pay the rent. An inexpensive means of making music was just what cash-strapped post-war Britain needed. The fact that some of these instruments were not too demanding on the players' musical talents was an added bonus.

Skiffle's British popularity is largely down to one man. Lonnie Donegan was the guitarist in Ken Colyer's jazz band (which would later evolve into the Chris Barber Band). He was allowed to play a couple of blues- or folk-based numbers as part of their live show, to give the other band members a rest, and they were generally well-received by the audience. So, when the new Chris Barber Band came to record their debut album in 1954, the tracks included Donegan's version of the Leadbelly song 'Rock Island Line'. Not everyone loved it – George Melly witheringly said that Donegan sounded more like George Formby than Leadbelly, and another critic described his voice as an 'energetic whine'. However, there was enough critical acclaim for it to be released as a single, and the song enjoyed twenty-two weeks in the charts, reaching number eight and selling 3 million copies. Significantly, and unusually for those days, most of the purchasers were young people.

Donegan went on to enjoy number one hits with 'Cumberland Gap' and the 'Battle of New Orleans', and was the inspiration for a thousand home-made skiffle groups up and down the country. One of these, the Quarrymen from Liverpool, would go on to become the Beatles, and members of the Rolling Stones, the Hollies and the Shadows all 'skiffled' at one time or another. Attempts by the television show *Six-Five Special* (of which more, shortly) to launch a skiffle contest ran into trouble with the Musicians' Union, precisely because most of the entrants would have been amateur musicians. Skiffle was at the height of its popularity around 1957, and Donegan had thirty-four hits between 1956 and 1962. As skiffle's appeal began to fade, Donegan became more of an all-round entertainer in the music hall tradition. His comedy song 'My Old Man's A Dustman' was a cleaned-up version of a ribald Liverpool folk song, and entered the charts at number one.

Skiffle was not entirely a one-man enterprise; Chas McDevitt and Nancy Whiskey had a big hit with 'Freight Train', and the Vipers Skiffle Group may be best remembered today for their singer/guitarist Wally Whyton. He made the transition into a children's television entertainer, where he shared the limelight with the puppets Pussy Cat Willum, Olly Beak and Fred Barker.

The cats are jumping – youth television

For much of the 1950s, the hour between 6 and 7 p.m. was known to the BBC as the 'toddler's truce' – a break in television transmission to enable parents to get young children to bed. This was discontinued in February 1957 and the BBC decided to fill the slot with something that would appeal to the younger generation, albeit not as young as toddlers. They brought in producer Jack Good to develop the format. The title was straightforward: the programme would follow a five-minute news bulletin that went out at 6 p.m., so it became the *Six-Five Special*, its title sequence featuring a speeding express train and the theme tune, originally played by the Bob Cort Skiffle Group:

'The Six-Five Special's coming down the line,
The Six-Five Special's right on time …'

The show was hosted by Pete Murray and Jo(sephine) Douglas (the latter was also its first producer). Murray, be-suited and looking to modern eyes prematurely middle-aged, was presumably the BBC's idea of someone who was 'down wiv de kids' (to borrow a more or less contemporary idiom that will soon sound as embarrassing as Murray's 'cool cats', 'time to jive on the old six-five' and 'giving us the gas'). Douglas actually found it necessary to supply excruciatingly scripted English translations for Murray's forays into teenage slang. There was tension from the start between Good and the BBC suits over the format of the show. The BBC wanted a magazine format, with a range of different types of music, interspersed with sports, public service and other items.

Despite Good throwing away the sets built for the programme to create room for the melee of dancers and performers that he wanted, the show went on. The former boxer Freddie Mills was brought in to do a sports item, Mike and Bernie Winters had a comedy spot, and there were things like a teeth-grinding appearance by a trendy vicar doing the hand jive, and even a short-lived classical music slot. So much for a show designed to woo young viewers with its beat, vitality, energy and (according to its detractors) wild abandon. The show was not as Jack Good had envisaged and he quit early in 1958. This did not stop the BBC suits from hating it, even in its watered-down form. For the first show, prizes of LP (for younger readers, Long Playing record) vouchers were given to the couple who 'cut the coolest' capers. Some female audience members found a sure-fire way of catching the judges' attention, leading one BBC executive to complain that 'there were too many girls who wore very abbreviated skirts, and several who wore practically no skirts at all'. Nonetheless, it proved hugely popular and was given an indefinite extension to its original six-week run.

Meanwhile, Good moved over to the commercial channel and created the show he had really wanted to produce. *Oh Boy!* went head to head with *Six-Five Special* from June 1958. *Oh Boy!* was much more hard-core rock and roll, with resident band Lord Rockingham's XI (who had their own number one hit with 'Hoots Mon'), the Vernon's Girls, Marty Wilde, Billy Fury and more or less all of the rock and roll aristocracy. Their first show discovered teenage sensation Cliff Richard, and helped to propel his song 'Move It' into the charts. Good had the satisfaction of trouncing *Six-Five Special* in the audience ratings, which gave the BBC executives just the excuse they needed for axing it. Having seen how superior a product *Oh Boy!* was, they instructed their programme makers to produce a BBC equivalent – but 'without cluttering up the studio and the screen with juvenile delinquents'. The result was called *Dig This!*

Oh Boy! itself only lasted until May 1959. Various other youth television formats followed with *Boy Meets Girls*, *Drumbeat* and so on, but the replacement of *Drumbeat* by *Juke Box Jury* in June 1959 – a programme that prided itself on having an audience aged between four and ninety-four – effectively marked the end of 1950s rock and roll.

1950s Food and 1950s Kitchens

*I*n this chapter, we look at what we were eating in the 1950s, how we cooked it, and some other related aspects of domestic life at that time.

Rationing

'I have no easy words for the nation. I cannot say when we will emerge into easier times.'

(Prime Minister Clement Attlee)

'At least we're not being bombed!'
   (A cheery view of rationing, more and more rarely heard after the war)

During the beginning of the 1950s, the one thing that dominated British eating habits more than any other was rationing. Before the war, Britain imported some 20 million tons of food a year – 50 per cent of our meat, 70 per cent of cheese and sugar, almost 80 per cent of our fruit and 70 per cent of cereals and fats. Hitler's submarine blockade of the islands made wartime rationing inevitable. Thanks to a combination of bad harvests, natural disasters, labour shortages on the farms, starvation across much of the post-war world and the nation's parlous economic state, rationing went on for a post-war period longer than the duration of the war itself, finally ending on 3 July 1954, a considerable

time after other western European countries, including our defeated enemies. In some cases, our post-war rations were even more restricted than in wartime.

Bread was rationed at one stage – something that had never happened during the war years – and so too were potatoes, between the autumn of 1947 and the end of April 1948. In 1951, the meat ration reached its lowest ever level after the end of the war due to a spat with one of our major meat suppliers – Argentina – over the Falkland Islands, as did that for cheese. Rationing, which had been grudgingly accepted as part of the war effort, became an increasing source of discontent after it. Particularly irritating was the bureaucratic and nit-picking way in which it was administered; in one case, a barrow-boy with a licence to sell vegetables was prosecuted for selling rhubarb (classed as a fruit). In restaurants, a serving of bread counted as a separate dish, at a time when only three dishes per diner were allowed (so bread lovers had to forego either starter or pudding). However, bread as part of a dish (say, cheese on toast) did not count separately.

The right-wing Housewives' League was established in 1945 as a means of articulating public discontent over rationing – in their view, it was an instrument of Communism. They collected a 500,000-signature petition against bread rationing and claimed credit for the Conservative election victory in 1951, which, they said, Labour lost in the queues for the butchers and grocers.

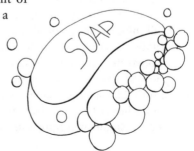

The timetable for the phasing out of rationing went as follows:

Bread – (first rationed in 1946) July 1948

Preserves – December 1948

Petrol – May 1950

Soap – September 1950

Goods with 'points' – May 1950

Tea, ham – October 1952

Sweets, chocolate – February 1953

Eggs – March 1953

Cream - April 1953

Sugar – September 1953

Butter, margarine, cooking fats, cheese – May 1954

Bacon, meat – July 1954

Not only did rationing affect the quantity of food available, it also influenced choice. Nowhere was this more clear than in the case of cheese. During the war, production was rationalised to just one product – what became known as 'government cheddar'. Nearly all other types of cheese production were phased out, and continuing government controls over milk supplies were still influencing the production of other varieties as late as the 1980s. Government attempts to fill shortages with alternative foodstuffs were not always crowned with success. One of the more spectacular failures was an unpalatable tinned fish from South Africa called snoek. Despite huge promotional efforts and a host of recipe ideas, by the summer of 1949 a third of the consignment shipped in during 1947 remained unsold. A renewed public relations campaign proved equally unavailing and, around the time of the Festival of Britain, suspiciously plentiful supplies of a new fishy cat food came on the market.

To give a flavour of what rationing really meant, here are the weekly (note, not daily) allowances per person in 1948, just before items began being removed from the ration:

Bacon/ ham – 1oz

Cheese – 1.5oz

Butter/ margarine – 7oz

Cooking fats – 2oz

Meat – 1 shilling (rationed by price, rather than weight)

Sugar – 8oz

Tea – 2oz

Chocolate/sweets – 4oz

Eggs – no fixed ration, just 'as available'

Milk – 3 pints

Preserves – 4oz

Food rationed by points – 4 points per week

... and after rationing?

As rationing gradually became just an unpleasant memory, the nation was able to spread its culinary wings (subject only to individuals' financial circumstances and the non-availability of some of the more exotic foodstuffs we take for granted today). Here is a selection of the foodstuffs that either came to prominence during the 1950s, or at least featured highly in the national diet. The first is not so much a foodstuff as a means of storing and distributing food that revolutionised our diets.

Frozen food sales took off spectacularly in the 1950s, despite the fact that only a tiny proportion of households had freezers, even by the end of the decade. Even without such an appliance, it meant that people could enjoy many more types of fruit, vegetables and fish out of season than before. In 1954, 100,000 packs of frozen food were sold in Britain; by 1960, this had risen to 360 million. 'As F-R-E-S-H as if you picked them in your own garden' the Birdseye advertisements used to boast. Their other big marketing slogan was 'No waste! You eat all you buy!' What they did not mention was that you also pay for the bits the factory throws away.

Mr Clarence Birdseye was an arctic fisherman who discovered that the fast freezing to which his catch was inevitably subject to preserved their taste and texture much better than a slower process. Blast freezing also made foods that were previously considered luxury items more affordable. Just 1 million chickens were sold in Britain in 1950, but this had increased to around 150 million by the 1960s. Frozen chickens had another bonus for the household without a fridge – if you put one next to the milk, it would keep it fresher for longer.

One frozen food product in particularly caught the public's imagination:

Fish fingers were originally developed in the United States by Clarence Birdseye in the 1920s, but it was in the 1950s, when the British fishing industry found itself with a glut of herrings, that it was decided they should be tried in Britain. Herring fish fingers (sold in the US as 'herring savouries') were test-marketed in Southampton and South Wales, using a much blander cod-based alternative as a basis for comparison. To everyone's surprise, the British palate preferred the cod variety, and it was this that went on the market (at 1*s* 8*d* [8p] a packet) in September 1955, just before the launch of commercial television. It was the workers at the Great Yarmouth factory where they were originally made who chose the name 'fish fingers', rejecting the alternative of 'battered cod pieces' (which may have carried distasteful Elizabethan overtones). Since then, we have not been able to get enough of them, with 15 billion disappearing down British throats to date.

TV dinners were another frozen delicacy associated with a period of ever-increasing television and refrigerator ownership. The credit (if credit is due) for their invention is somewhat shrouded in mystery. As we saw, the fast freezing technology essential to their production was perfected by Clarence Birdseye back in the 1920s. Another company invented the compartmentalised tray in which they are served, though these were at first only sold to organisations like the military and Pan American Airways, rather than on the open retail market. Yet a third company brought the two ideas together and started retailing frozen meals in foil trays in a relatively small way, but it was an American firm of poultry producers called Swanson who popularised them and invented the brand name (it was originally called the 'TV Brand Frozen Dinner'). It all happened because, in 1953, they seriously over-estimated the demand for poultry at Thanksgiving and were left with about 250 tons of surplus birds on their hands. To get rid of them, they tried the frozen dinner experiment, hoping to sell

about 5,000 in the first year; in fact, they sold 10 million and the convenience meal was well and truly up and running. They took considerably longer to catch on over here, but Britain is now truly hooked, devouring £18 billion worth of convenience meals each year.

Spam is unwanted e-mail traffic to the internet generation, but, long before that, it was a portmanteau word used to describe spiced ham – a canned pre-cooked meat product developed in America before the Second World War. It was imported to Britain in large quantities during the war (not least in American troops' rations) and formed an important part of the nation's diet, both during the war years and for a long time afterwards. In addition to meat, it contained salt, water, potato starch and a sodium nitrate preservative, and was for many post-war years made under licence in Liverpool. It could go into sandwiches, salads, stews and a host of other meals, but one of the favourite ways of presenting it was the spam fritter – a nutritionist's nightmare of a battered, deep-fried slice of the product. Be still, my beating heart attack!

Coronation chicken is a dish whose very name links it with the 1950s. One of the problems facing the organisers of the coronation was how to feed the 300 guests that were being invited to the coronation luncheon. It was a florist, Constance Spry, who was often credited with the idea of cold pre-cooked chicken, served in a mayonnaise sauce flavoured with apricots and curry powder (the latter used in lieu of any more subtle blend of herbs and spices, many of which were unavailable at the time). In fact, Spry worked with chef Rosemary Hume, and both of them had to obtain the consent of the Ministry of Works for their menu. The dish had its antecedent in Jubilee Chicken, a very similar recipe served at George V's Jubilee in 1935. In addition to being deemed fit for the Queen's royal guests, the lack of last-minute preparation involved made it ideal for a million of her couch-potato subjects on coronation day, who did not wish to miss a moment of the televised ceremony. Although it contained curry powder, to call it a curry would certainly be overstating the case. Constance Spry spoke of it having more of a 'delicate nut-like flavour'.

A reminder of some other delicacies of the period

Prawn cocktail: peeled prawns in a sauce of plain yogurt, mayonnaise, Worcestershire sauce, tomato ketchup, horseradish, and lemon juice.

French onion soup: onion soup made with beef stock, grated cheese, sherry, and a hint of garlic, topped with slices of French bread.

Steak Diane: steak served in a sauce of onions, Worcestershire sauce, lemon juice and parsley.

Chicken Maryland: chicken joints fried in breadcrumbs and served with fried bananas or corn fritters.

Lemon meringue pie: an open pie, filled with a mixture of lemon juice, cornflour, sugar, egg yolks and nutmeg, topped with a meringue made of egg whites and caster sugar. (Particularly popular when eggs were no longer rationed.)

Pineapple upside-down pudding: tinned pineapple, glacé cherries, covered in a floury sugary mixture, baked and served – as its name suggests – upside down.

Black Forest Gateau: a gooey confection of chocolate cake, black cherries and cream. (A more decadent version included cherry liquor).

Takeaways and eating out

Today, fast food and eating out consumes a sizeable part of our food budget, but at the start of the 1950s the term 'takeaway' was almost exclusively reserved for the traditional fish and chip shop. The days of Chinese and Indian takeaways in every town were still some way off, and McDonalds would not licence their first American franchise until April 1955. Pizza – described as 'Italian Welsh rarebit' for the benefit of an uncomprehending nation – was making its first tentative appearance in the country. However, the first wave of American-style dining reached us in the mid-1950s, as Wimpy Bars began to appear in our high streets. At the time, it was felt that a word or two of explanation was needed in the local press for the British consumer:

> What is a Wimpy?
> A pure beef hamburger that has the reputation of being a meal in itself. It has found favour in London's West End – and in Buckingham Palace. The Queen offered Wimpys to her guests at an important reception recently.

No doubt the Royals were still strapped for cash after the expense of the coronation and, at 1*s* 3*d* (6p) a time, Wimpys made good economic sense for them (in the unlikely event that the advertisers were to be believed). By the end of the 1960s, Britain could boast 460 Wimpy Bars. Another important chain of restaurants, the Berni Inns, was launched, starting in Bristol, at about the same time – but offered a more conservative menu, with a half-pound steak, chips, peas, roll and butter, and a choice of pudding or cheese, all for 7*s* 6*d* (37p).

Another foreign influence on our diet was the coffee bar. Achille Gaggia invented his espresso coffee machine in 1938, but the distractions of the Second World War prevented it being marketed until 1946. From about 1953 onwards, coffee bars became the places for young people to be seen, and a 'frothing creamy drink' called cappuccino began to displace the traditional cup of tea in their affections. Despite the Italian origins of their hardware, coffee bars were seen as another example of the American influence taking over in our society – what one American diplomat called the 'Coca-Colonisation' of Britain. There were some 2,000 coffee bars by 1960, but they tended to disappear as swiftly as they had sprung up, as their owners realised that there was not much money to be made out of teenagers eking out one cup of coffee for hours. Many got food licences and became Italian restaurants.

Brands

In the traditional pre-war grocer's shop, much of your order was assembled from the raw materials. Sugar was measured out from a sack, bacon cut on a lethal-looking slicer, cheese cut with a wire and portions of butter patted into shape with little wooden paddles. Clearly, such arrangements would never work in the new generation of self-service stores, and the fifties were characterised by a move towards pre-packaged and branded goods. Here, we look at some examples of the treats that became available to us and the ways in which the advertisers sought to sell them, particularly as the seller's market brought about by rationing gradually disappeared and the introduction of commercial television gave a whole new dimension to the marketing of foodstuffs.

One approach was to hark back to the supposedly halcyon pre-war days before rationing. Thus, Camp coffee promised to be 'the same as pre-war', as they faced growing competition from Nescafé (which doubled its sales in the decade after the war) and a newcomer, Maxwell House. In similar vein, brewers boasted of their beers returning to pre-war strength. Quite the opposite approach was taken by the makers of Summer County margarine. Although rationing of margarine was ended in May 1954, Summer County did not come onto the market until November of that year, by which time it could claim to be 'the first margarine to be planned after the end of all rationing and restrictions'. The hope was that it would stand it apart from traditional margarines, which in the war years did not have the best of reputations. No such delays for their rivals Stork, who ran teaser-adverts in the weeks leading up to the end of margarine rationing:

'Only four weeks to wait for Stork margarine ... one taste and you'll know what you've been missing ...'

'A fortnight's not long to wait – except when you're waiting for your first taste of Stork after fourteen dreary years of making do. Or rather, your first taste ever!'

Another hangover from the war years was the way in which products offered to soothe fraught nerves. Wrigleys chewing gum was one which had long promised to ease tension. Another way to relax was to be permanently sozzled. Advertisers in the 1950s could take a rather more cavalier attitude to promoting the health-giving properties of alcohol than their modern counterparts. Hall's wine was apparently enriched with vitamins, others described themselves as medicated or tonic wines, while Keystone burgundy offered readers this little vignette:

> This bank manager, ill from over-work, took Keystone on his doctor's recommendation, and subsequently always took it when he needed a pick-me-up … Yes, doctors know the value of good burgundy when you are run-down, over-tired, weakened from illness.

> The advertisement stopped short only of showing the befuddled bank manager throwing his arms round his customers and crying 'I ***** love you!' to them all.

One difficult sell in the days before widespread refrigerator ownership was ice cream. The best Walls could manage with its 'family bricks' was telling people that, 'wrapped in newspaper before you leave the shop, Walls stays firm for two to three hours.' After that, you could always drink it.

Tinned goods were some of the earliest convenience products, and the advertisers did not hesitate to trumpet their superiority, even over the real thing: 'Lin-Can fresh is preferable to the staleness of so-called "fresh".' They also sought to appeal to a whole generation of young housewives, who were generally assumed to be clueless about cookery. One brand of tinned fruit boasted that 'it all adds up to chef cookery – but well within the scope of even a young bride'. One of the barriers any new convenience food had to overcome was the guilt of the 1950s housewife who had not painstakingly prepared the meal from scratch. Batchelors' dried packet soups addressed this head-on in their 1956 advertisement, telling the customer, 'If you pride yourself on serving [freshly-cooked] food, warming up just isn't good enough.' By their definition, adding the water to their product and simmering it meant that 'you actually COOK the food yourself' and 'you serve it freshly made'.

Celebrity chefs and foreign food

Today, the media gives us wall-to-wall coverage of celebrity chefs. In the immediate post-war period, the fledgling television service had Philip Harben and Marguerite Patten as their cookery experts, though the latter rejected any suggestion of celebrity:

> Philip Harben and I weren't celebrities. We were informers, much less important than the food. Our role during rationing was to guide people through interesting meals when what you could buy was so limited.

For his part, Harben tried to get the British public to be (ever so slightly) more adventurous with its diet. However, his television programme *Continental Cooking* got a poor reception from the public, as he tried to wean them onto such exotica as French onion soup and 'pasta from Italy'. The BBC's Viewing Panel told him he should give them 'more everyday dishes'.

No suggestion of modesty or the mundane was evident in the television programmes of cooks Fanny and Johnny Cradock. Dressed as if they were on their way to a state banquet, the terrifying Fanny would conjure up recipes of Byzantine complexity and heart-stopping calorific value, whilst the monocled Johnny hovered in the background, getting in the way and being unmercifully bullied by her. However, television audiences seemed to like watching them (possibly in the hope that Johnny would one day rise up against his tormenter and beat her to death with a wooden spoon).

Another person who is credited with being hugely influential in raising the standard of British cuisine is Elizabeth David, with her books including *Mediterranean Food* (1950) and *French*

Country Cooking (1951). David was from an upper-class background (the debutante daughter of a Conservative MP and grand-daughter of a viscount) but she rebelled, trying her hand at acting, painting and adultery before settling on cooking as her chosen means of support. However, it is questionable how much real impact her books had when first published, since many of the ingredients she listed were at that point unobtainable in Britain. They were books that were read with yearning rather than actually used – pornography for foodies. David came into her own in the 1960s, by which time her books had been reprinted by Penguin and the necessary ingredients were starting to appear in the shops.

Probably more widely influential in the 1950s was Bee Nilson, a domestic science teacher at North London Polytechnic. Her *Penguin Cookery Book* (1952) sold in large numbers. One not entirely uncritical review said that it 'treated food like domestic science' and that, whilst practical, 'if followed carefully, [it] will give plain and edible results but, I imagine, little enjoyment' – which just about sums up much of British catering in the 1950s. At its worst (even in supposedly superior establishments), British catering was even more terrible than this – meat overcooked, vegetables boiled to within an inch of their lives and sodden with water, either totally unseasoned or peppered and salted to death, and with packaged or tinned products being passed off (unconvincingly) as homemade.

Britain's imperial connections meant that the nation had long been aware of the cuisines of other nations. For example, Mrs Beeton's Victorian book of household management contained a variety of curry recipes. However, after fourteen years of rationing, food shortages and the long working hours imposed by the war, there was a whole generation of housewives who were not used to taking on anything beyond the plainest of plain cooking. Foreign food had to be reintroduced. Thus, *Good Housekeeping* magazine was to be found, in 1953, explaining what pasta was and the variety of different shapes in which it came: 'Even if you have no access to an Italian shop and cannot buy the wide variety of pasta shown in our photograph, ordinary macaroni is easily obtainable everywhere and tastes just as good as the more fancy shapes.'

At this time, the only way many households knew to cook with pasta was macaroni cheese.

English recipe: boil the macaroni until over-cooked, cover it in a sauce made of milk thickened with flour and the merest hint of cheddar, then bake it in an oven for an hour or so.

Hard labour in the kitchen

One reason why the 1950s housewife might find it difficult to indulge in flights of culinary fancy was all the other domestic demands on their time. The lot of the typical housewife in 1950 was not a happy one. They had few of the labour-saving devices their modern counterparts take for granted and contemporary studies showed that they typically worked a seventy-five-hour week. It was hard work, too; Mass Observation carried out one experiment which showed that doing housework could typically consume seventy-five calories in fifteen minutes – the equivalent of an aerobic workout.

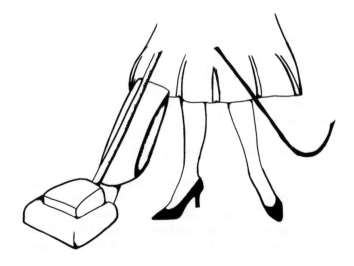

Many domestic chores had to be done the hard way. Before the vacuum cleaner, you swept the carpets and, in order not to spread dust, you were advised to cover the furniture with dustsheets each time. The burners on your gas stove would need regular cleaning in a solution of soda, finishing them off with a paraffin and turpentine solution. Dry cleaning might be done at home, using petrol (well away from any open fires!) or fuller's earth.

Labour-saving gadgets

The fifties were the decade when many more people acquired the labour-saving devices that had hitherto been the exclusive property of the rich. The following table shows a comparison between 1946 and 1965 of the percentage of households with each appliance:

	1946	1965
Vacuum cleaner	32	81
Electric iron	65	94
Electric cooker	16	35
Telephone	21	35
Television	0.25	85
Fridge	2.1	46
Freezer	0	3
Microwave	0	1
Washing machine	3	58
Dishwasher	0.01	1.5
Food mixer	0.1	11
Electric fire	57	70
Immersion heater	12	45

(www.makingthemodernworld.org.uk)

Even some of the so-called labour-saving appliances were harder work than their modern counterparts are. If you were one of the few who had a washing machine, and you lived in a hard water area in the days before water softeners, you faced the build-up of a scum deposit that had to be rinsed off with a brush moistened with paraffin, and then rinsed out with clean warm water and soap. Fridges might need to be defrosted every fortnight and you would need to oil their bearings.

For quite a few households, one limiting factor on the use of gadgets would have been the lack of a suitable power supply. Before 1937 and the opening of a National Grid, there had not even been a standard voltage across the nation. In 1946, only around 80 per cent of households had electric lighting, and a number of those who did have an electricity supply would not have had separate power sockets, or had sockets that were grossly deficient in number, non-standard or unsafe in some way. Appliances might need up to three different types of plug and ten different types of fuse. It was only in 1950 that national regulations were introduced, to standardise fittings and make ring mains compulsory.

The war changed a lot of attitudes about women (in particular married women) working and any idea that they would be prepared to revert to pre-war domesticity once the fighting ended proved to be ill-founded. In 1947, just 18 per cent of married women were in work, but this rose to 33 per cent by 1957 and 50 per cent by 1961. The additional income that wives brought into the household was one of the factors that enabled them to buy the gadgets (and the fact that they were out of the house at work no doubt made it essential that they had them).

Washday was a major demand on a housewife's time when her only labour-saving devices were the mangle and the washboard. The twin-tub washing machine began to make its appearance in the 1950s, but it still had to be wheeled out for each use and plumbed into the sink. More to the point, they could cost around £95, a sum for which you could buy a small car.

There were those looking to make domestic appliances more affordable – notably John Bloom, who was born in London's East End in 1931 and whose motto was 'It's no sin to make a profit'. After National Service, he began selling washing machines door-to-door, until he decided he could do better working for himself. He managed to source a supply of Dutch-made twin-tub washing machines, which he was able to sell through a combination of home demonstrations and direct advertising (he started placing ads in the *Daily Mirror* in 1958) for 39 guineas (£40.90) – about half the price of his nearest rival. Not surprisingly, he was soon selling 500 a week (about 10 per cent of the overall market), largely financed through the Government's relaxation of the hire purchase regulations. He further cut his costs by buying up the moribund Rolls Razor company and giving them a contract to build 25,000 machines.

Shortly after, he diversified into dishwashers and refrigerators, buying up the Colston and Prestcold companies in the process, and even struck a deal with the Communist Bulgarian Government, whereby he promoted their country as a new package-holiday destination, with two-week all-inclusive holidays for £59. By the end of 1963, he was selling over 200,000 machines a year – but he was running out of customers. This, and a price war launched by his rivals at about the same time, eventually led to the voluntary liquidation of his company in 1964 and his own bankruptcy in 1969. In the meantime, he had done much to free up what had been a suppliers' market, putting the customer much more in the driving seat.

Shopping was another big drain on a housewife's time. Even by the mid-1950s only about one in ten households had a refrigerator, which meant that shopping for perishables had to

be done on a more or less daily basis. Housewives would spend an average of ten hours a week shopping. Price was again a major consideration – a 1950s refrigerator would have cost the equivalent in modern money of £1,200. It was not until the Budget of 1958, when purchase tax was halved and restrictions on hire purchase removed (who would have guessed that an election was in prospect?), that sales really took off, with 400,000 being bought by the end of the year.

One by one, other labour-saving kitchen appliances made their appearance. Mr Morphy got together with Mr Richards and gave us a machine that would toast both sides of the bread at once; Mr Russell met Mr Hobbs and begat the electric kettle, and Mr Kenneth Wood did not get together with anyone, but joined his names together to produce the Kenwood Chef food-mixer. Again, these were not initially cheap appliances: a Kenwood Chef would cost around £20 at a time when the average annual wage was around £600.

Protest

*I*n this chapter, we look at a range of protests that marked the 1950s.

Suez

This represents one of the shortest-lived movements in the history of protest, but one that saw its objectives achieved (though not through any action that the domestic protesters themselves took).

Ever since its opening in 1869, the Suez Canal had formed a vital link between Britain and its trading interests in the east. From 1882, the British government installed a garrison in Egypt to protect their interests following nationalist riots, and for the next seventy years, Egypt effectively became a British possession. Certainly, the British treated the 'wogs' (as they referred to the locals) as if they were their colonial masters. This was not well received by the Egyptians and their discontent boiled over in 1952, in a gunfight between British troops and Egyptian police that left fifty dead and one hundred wounded, and led to riots in Cairo, killing thirty more.

That same year saw the overthrow of the corrupt Egyptian King Farouk and, by 1956, the presidency rested with an ambitious army officer, Colonel Gamal Abdel Nasser. His increasing alignment with the Communist bloc led Britain to withdraw an offer of funding towards Nasser's pet project, the Asswan Dam, in July 1956. Nasser duly bridged the funding gap Britain had created by seizing and nationalising the Canal. Foreign (and potentially hostile) control of the Canal could have crippled Britain, a quarter of whose imports and 80 per cent of whose oil then came through it.

Back at home, Prime Minister Anthony Eden was about a year into his term, and was already facing rumblings of discontent from within his own party and the nation at large. These held that he was a weak prime minister, appeasing the Socialists at home and the Arabs abroad. Back in the 1930s, Eden had resigned from the government of the day over Chamberlain's policy of appeasing Hitler, and his personal standing had benefited enormously from that stand. Like much of the nation, Eden was outraged by the actions of the 'tin-pot little dictator', Nasser, so there was a strong domestic agenda for firm British action over the nationalisation.

However, the world would not have liked Britain just wielding the big stick as the neo-colonial bully, so, after some delay, a highly secret plan was hatched to have Egypt's sworn enemy, Israel, attack them. Once they had achieved their military objectives, an Anglo-French force would then move into Egypt, ostensibly as peacekeepers, and make the two sides retreat from the Canal Zone, which they would then 'protect'.

It was vital that America go along with this plan (in which they were not fellow conspirators), not so much for military reasons but because Britain was, at that time, in a balance of payments crisis. They needed a loan from the International Monetary Fund to get them out of trouble, and this would only be achieved with American support. However, the British timing could not have been worse; the Anglo-French force went in just a week before the US Presidential elections. American public opinion was strongly against any kind of foreign war that might entangle them in any way. International opinion was largely against the Anglo-French plan and the United Nations instead proposed a UN peacekeeping force – one that did not involve Britain or France.

Domestic public opinion was split right down the middle. After the initial jingoistic outbursts, enthusiasm for conflict waned. An anti-war protest meeting in Trafalgar Square, on 4 November 1956, attracted a crowd of 30,000. One attendee, who had gone simply out of curiosity, was the Prime Minister's wife, Clarissa. She was recognised and cheered for what the demonstrators took to be her support for their cause. She fled back to Downing Street, from where the baying of the mob could still be heard. Finally, the Americans forced the British hand – they would only back the IMF loan if the British withdrew from Egypt. Sterling could not have survived without the loan, and so the government was forced into a humiliating climb-down.

This debacle finished Eden as Prime Minister. His health had always been fragile, following a series of major operations, but the stresses of the crisis left him a broken man, unable to continue in the role. He disappeared off to Jamaica for a long convalescence, something that also did not go down well with the British public while the British troops were still stuck in Egypt. As Randolph Churchill put it, Hitler had refused to withdraw his troops from Stalingrad, but even Hitler did not then winter in Jamaica. When Eden finally returned home, one caustic newspaper headline read 'PRIME MINISTER VISITS BRITAIN'. Eden resigned in January 1957, and went off for a recuperative cruise to New Zealand, where he had some interesting discussions with his cabin steward – one John Prescott, the future Labour Deputy Prime Minister.

Suez significantly brought home to the nation the reality of post-war Britain as a world power. It was later said by *Private Eye* of another Conservative Prime Minister that he had the perfect background for the job – Eton, Oxford, Munich and Suez. The same could be said of Eden, except he at least resigned over appeasement – and Suez.

Committee for Nuclear Disarmament

By the latter part of the 1950s, there was growing concern about the threat posed to the world by nuclear weapons. Ownership of them seemed to be spreading, and attempts to negotiate multi-lateral disarmament in the context of the Cold War seemed to be going nowhere. In November 1957, the *New Statesman* published an article by J.B. Priestley, 'Britain and the Nuclear Bombs'. In particular, it was critical of the Labour politician Aneurin Bevan's change of heart about supporting unilateral disarmament. The article attracted an unexpectedly large volume of support, and the following February, led to a meeting at the Central Hall, Westminster, attended by some 5,000 people, at which the Campaign for Nuclear Disarmament was formed. Canon John Collins of St Paul's Cathedral was its first chairman, and many of the great and the good from different walks of public life registered their support.

That Easter, a protest march was organised from London to the government's atomic weapons research establishment at Aldermaston in Berkshire – subsequent marches went in the opposite direction. This became an annual event that, in 1959 attracted 60,000 protesters and, by 1961, 150,000. The organisation was always multi-facetted in its approach. Some parts sought to effect change through mainstream political processes, and in 1960 they were successful in persuading the Labour Party to adopt a policy of unilateralism. (Labour leader Hugh Gaitskell was always strongly opposed to the policy. He vowed to 'fight, fight and fight again' to have it reversed. In the end, he only had to 'fight', the policy being overturned in 1961.) Others wanted more direct action, and, in 1960, the veteran philosopher Bertrand Russell set up the 'Committee of 100' to organise a programme of non-violent direct action. They arranged things like a sit-down demonstration outside the Ministry of Defence and another protest meeting in Trafalgar Square that led to 1,300 demonstrators being arrested.

The organisation's choice of logo was to become one of the most universally known symbols. Designed by Gerald Holtom, it was based on the semaphore symbols for the letters 'N' and 'D' (for nuclear disarmament). The other inspiration for it was said to be a painting by Goya, of a man with his arms stretched downwards and outwards in a gesture of despair. The logo was never copyrighted and its use spread throughout the peace movement.

CND was always seen as middle-class radicalism, whose core backing was with Labour supporters. As such, it was regarded as deeply suspicious by parts of the establishment. Various bodies were set up to try to counter its influence; some (like the British Atlantic Committee) got government funding, and some were not above the use of dirty tricks to achieve their ends. During the 1960s, MI5 classified CND as 'Communist-controlled'. The world would experience its closest brush with nuclear Armageddon with the Cuban missile crisis of 1962, but the Test Ban Treaty the following year led to something of a dip in support for CND. At no stage did more than one in four of the population support unilateral nuclear disarmament.

Immigration and the Notting Hill riots

Before the Second World War, most parts of Britain (apart from a few of our seaports) had scarcely seen a black face. The first encounter many Britons had with them were the large numbers of black GIs who came to Britain in the run-up to D-Day, and much of Britain was shocked by the prejudice shown towards them by some of their white American compatriots. In addition, there was a significant influx of black Commonwealth troops – some 7,000 West Indians joined the RAF, for example.

After the war, one of the government's responses to labour shortages in areas like transport and the new Health Service was to encourage the immigration of suitably skilled people from the so-called black Commonwealth, many of whom faced high levels of unemployment in their own country. The first significant influx arrived on a former Nazi cruise ship, the *Empire Windrush*, in June 1948, but, until the 1950s, immigration was generally on a small scale – less than a thousand a year. The 1951 Census put the country's total Afro-Caribbean population at no more than 20,900 and this only grew to 24,200 by 1953. It was in the latter part of the 1950s that the rate increased dramatically. Some 161,450 were estimated to have arrived between 1955 and 1960, and the 1966 Census recorded 454,100 West Indians and 50,700 West Africans (though some of these would have been the children of immigrants, and were born here).

There may have been jobs here for the new arrivals, but little consideration was given to housing them. They could not afford to buy, did not qualify for Council housing, and many were forced into the private rented sector, where they faced either blatant prejudice ('no dogs, no Irish, no blacks'), covert prejudice ('sorry, the flat's already been taken' – when it had not) or unscrupulous landlords like the notorious Peter Rachman. These property owners forced their tenants to pay exorbitant rents for overcrowded, squalid accommodation, and the immigrants found themselves competing for housing with some of the poorest elements of the white population. In addition, the tension likely to exist in any impoverished community took on a racial dimension with noise and other nuisances from West Indian clubs, and some members of that community living off the proceeds of vice.

Although the troubles of August/September 1958 are referred to as the Notting Hill race riots, they actually began in Nottingham, and their first manifestation in Notting Hill was an attack by white youths on a Swedish woman, Majbritt Morrison. She turned on the gang of nine youths when they started racially abusing her Jamaican husband. The next night, they tracked her down and beat her with stones, planks of wood and an iron bar. The police rescued her and the culprits were arrested within twenty-four hours, later receiving 'exemplary' four-year prison sentences. Later that night, gangs of white youths totalling some 300 to 400 roamed the streets, smashing up West Indian homes and attacking any black people that they came across. The attacks continued nightly until 5 September, and parts of the West Indian community responded by also going out armed, either for self-defence or to confront the rioters and attack known bases of racist groups.

During the course of the riots, 140 people were arrested, and 108 were charged with violent offences or the carrying of arms – 72 of them white, 36 black. Both sides complained about their treatment at the hands of the police, but confidential government papers, only released in 2002, show that senior policemen had tried to persuade the Home Secretary that there was little or no racist dimension to the riots – that it was simply 'ruffians both coloured and white' hell-bent on hooliganism. It was said that their treatment during the riots contributed to the on-going suspicion of the police by parts of the West Indian community.

The tensions were undoubtedly fanned by Oswald Mosley's far-right Union Movement and the racist White Britain Group, who moved into the Notting Hill area. Mosley, in what was to be his last real bid for political influence, had his supporters distribute leaflets and held street corner meetings, in which he accused the blacks of stealing white homes and jobs, and exploiting white women in unspeakable ways. During the riots themselves, it was said that the far-right groups bussed in their supporters as *agents provocateurs*, to promote violence. However, it did them little good. When Mosley stood as a candidate for the constituency at the next General Election he came last, with just 8 per cent of the vote.

Angry young men...

British theatre-going in the early 1950s was a predominantly middle-class, middle-aged activity, for which one wore dinner jackets and cocktail dresses. Its leading playwrights were people like Noel Coward and Terence Rattigan, whose characters were for the most part frightfully middle or upper class, their emotions tightly buttoned up and their upper lips so stiff as to make them virtually incomprehensible. Politics and sex did not feature prominently in their plays (perhaps because both playwrights were – at that time illegally – homosexual?).

In May 1956, into this world stepped a failed actor turned playwright named John Osborne. The central character in his play *Look Back in Anger* (staged at the Royal Court Theatre) was Jimmy Porter, a working-class graduate who, for some reason, has chosen to run a sweet shop. He lives in a small flat in the Midlands with his upper-class wife, Alison, and a mutual friend, Cliff, both of whom he bullies unmercifully. They are later joined by an actress friend, Helena, creating a ménage á trois, in which Cliff tries to keep the peace. The play was strongly autobiographical – Osborne had just undergone a messy separation from his upper-class wife.

For reasons which were not entirely clear to all those who saw it, Jimmy was not a happy bunny. Nor were they any clearer about his prescription for the ills of the world. Class conflict is hinted at, without – in the eyes of its critics – being adequately explored, and they found a strand of misogyny that struck them as pre-feminist. Verdicts on Porter vary from him having 'a startling potency as the representative of a generation of disaffected British youth', through 'a man driven to madness by the unresponsive cool of those around him', to 'a self-pitying sentimentalist.'

One thing the play did not fail to do was to divide opinion. The most feared theatrical impresario of the day was Binkie Beaumont, who walked out of the premiere part of the way through. Osborne, whose specialist subject was abuse with little regard for who it was directed at, referred to 'Binkiedom' as 'the most powerful of the unacceptable faeces of theatrical capitalism'. Most of the critics hated it, with the exception of two of the most powerful, Kenneth Tynan and Harold Hobson, who were its passionate supporters. Tynan said, 'I could not love anyone who did not wish to see *Look Back in Anger*', and Hobson called it 'a landmark in British theatre'. The play was later transferred to Broadway, where it was nominated for three Tony awards, including best play, and was filmed three times. The first film, in 1959, starred Richard Burton and got four BAFTA nominations. It was also brilliantly satirised by Tony Hancock in *Look Back in Hunger*, by John Eastbourne. From it came the concept of the angry young man and the kitchen-sink drama, using harsh realism as an antidote to the blandness of mainstream theatre.

The term 'angry young man' was coined by the press officer at the Royal Court to publicise Osborne's play, but a lazy press used it as a blanket term to cover a host of playwrights and authors who were felt to be disillusioned in some way with traditional British society. The trouble was, many of them had little or nothing in common – they differed in their politics, their class backgrounds and in all sorts of other ways. They were also angry about different things, and some denied being angry about anything. Many of them cordially loathed each other, and so, as a protest movement, they made little sense and the term only remained at the forefront of journalistic interest for a few months, but by then it had taken root in the English language.

But, love it or hate it, *Look Back in Anger* had kicked down some theatrical doors. Perhaps it was Osborne's fellow playwrights and authors who were most aware of he had done. Arnold Wesker said that he 'opened the doors of theatres for all the succeeding generations of writers', and Alan Sillitoe said that Osborne 'did not just contribute to British theatre, he set off a landmine and blew most of it up'.

... and rebels without causes

James Dean was just twenty-six years old when he suffered a fatal car accident in his Porsche, near Los Angeles, in September 1955. He had made only three films, of which the third, *Giant*, would not be released until after his death, but Dean had already developed a reputation for playing variously mixed-up or misunderstood characters. His supporting role in *Giant*, as an older Texas oilman named Jeff Rink, was deliberately chosen to stop him being typecast in such roles.

Dean did not have the easiest of childhoods. His mother, to whom he was very close and who was said to be the only one who really understood him, died when he was nine. He was then sent from his home in Santa Monica, California, to live with Quaker relatives on a farm in Indiana. He took up acting whilst at the University College Los Angeles, and shortly afterwards dropped out to pursue it as a full-time career. He found his way to the prestigious Actors' Studio in New York, where he landed the part of a disaffected youth in a television play – ideal preparation for the roles that were to make him famous.

In *East of Eden*, the adaptation of the John Steinbeck book, he played Cal Trask, described as an 'angst-ridden protagonist and misunderstood outcast, desperately craving approval from a father figure'. Much of the action in this film was unscripted and Dean's performance earned him an Oscar nomination. From there, he went on to play Jim Stark in *Rebel Without a Cause*, a film that was hugely popular with young people for its portrayal of teenage angst.

Dean had a long-standing interest in motor sport and his acting income enabled him to buy a series of ever-faster motor cars and motorcycles. This culminated in a Porsche 550 Speedster, which he christened 'Little Bastard', and which Warner Brothers forbad him to race whilst filming for them. However, between films he liked to compete and was driving the Porsche to a race meeting on the day he died. He had already picked up one speeding ticket on the journey when his Porsche was involved in a head-on collision with another car on Route 466. The inquest reached a verdict of accidental death, and held that neither driver had committed any offence (something that may have been of more interest to the other driver, who survived). Dean had just completed a public safety film, warning people about speeding on the public highway. He told them, 'The life you save may be your own – the life you save may be mine.'

Dean joined the iconic club of public figures who will never grow old (in 2011 he should have celebrated his eightieth birthday) and has continued to exercise a strong grip on the public imagination. Even today, the Dean estate still earns around $5 million a year.

Andy Warhol tried to sum up Dean's appeal: 'He is not our hero because he is perfect, but because he perfectly represented the damaged but beautiful soul of our time.'

The Space Race

Russia vs America (and Germany?)

To many people, the exploration of space was the defining feature of both the 1950s and the decade that was to follow, and at the centre of it was a man with what we will neutrally call an interesting past. Wernher von Braun (1912–1977) had been fascinated by rockets from an early age, and in 1938 became the technical director of the Peenemunde military rocket establishment in Nazi Germany. He had been a member of the Nazi party since 1937, but his main interest seems to have been in the scientific use of rocketry for space exploration, rather than its military applications. Nonetheless, it was the latter that the Nazi hierarchy required, and von Braun gave them the V1 and V2 terror weapons.

By 1945, Peenemunde lay in the path of the Soviet advance into Germany and von Braun found himself facing contradictory sets of orders as the Soviet guns came within hearing range – one set told him to stay and defend the establishment to the last man, and the other to move out and stop all their secrets falling into Soviet hands. Von Braun and his colleagues chose the latter and, helped by a senior Nazi Hans Kammler (who hoped to use the scientists as a bargaining counter for his own life), found their way to the American lines.

By this time, both the Americans and Russians knew of von Braun's role in the war and both wanted to get their hands on him. Many thought that he and his colleagues ought to be tried for war crimes, in particular for the appalling concentration camp conditions in which slave labourers, who died in their thousands, were made to implement the V-weapons programme; the Americans, however, were more interested in von Braun's technical expertise because it was so much more advanced. Under conditions of great secrecy, von Braun and about 150 others were relocated to the United States. By the time news of this broke in the American press, the authorities were locked in the Cold War and were able to justify the Germans' technical expertise as being vital to staying one step ahead of the Russians. The Americans had their own rocket testing range in New Mexico and, as early as 1946, had been working on an intercontinental missile, the *Atlas*, which would later be developed to carry many of their early space missions.

The Americans may have won the race to secure German expertise, but it was Russia that won the race into space. On 4 October 1957, the Americans learned that the first Russian satellite, *Sputnik* (which means 'fellow traveller'), was flying over their airspace. The news traumatised the West; as long ago as 1943, British scientist R.V. Jones had warned that a missile would be capable of carrying a (then still to be invented) atomic bomb. Other possibilities, such as spy satellites, were also starting to be appreciated. *Sputnik* was a crude contraption, carrying nothing more than a radio device that enabled it to be tracked, and it only stayed in orbit for ninety-two days, but the symbolism was enormous. The *New York Times* spoke of 'a race for survival' and Russian leader Nikita Khrushchev hardly helped American paranoia when he spoke (in the context of a subsequent *Sputnik* launch) of America sleeping under a Soviet moon.

Things were to get worse. In November 1957, a second, much larger *Sputnik* was launched, this time carrying a dog, Laika (Laika only survived for about six hours, but the Soviets kept quiet about this). It is often thought that Laika was the first living creature to go into space, but this dubious honour goes to some fruit flies, which the Americans launched in a captured German V2 rocket in February 1947. They were even returned to ground safely, which is more than can be said for some of the mice, guinea pigs, hamsters, cats, dogs and monkeys sent up on subsequent excursions by the Americans in the late 1940s and early 1950s.

In December, America planned to launch its first satellite, *Explorer I*. They made the mistake of televising the event live. The rocket rose about 2ft from its launching pad, then fell back to the ground and exploded in a ball of flames. The satellite itself fell off and landed on the ground, from where it started to transmit. The press had a field day, variously calling it 'flopnik', 'dudnik' and 'kaputnik'. It would be the end of January 1958 before national pride was assuaged and the replacement started transmitting from space.

Von Braun survived American investigations into both his alleged Nazi and Communist sympathies, gained American citizenship, and was given a senior position in the American Space Agency

NASA, when President Eisenhower set it up in April 1958. He died in 1977, greatly honoured as an all-American hero.

The rest of the story is both well known and outside the scope of a book about the 1950s. The Apollo programme (announced in 1961) led to man setting foot on the moon in 1969, but not before mankind came as close as it has ever been to global destruction in 1962, in a cold war dispute about (what else?) missiles.

The British Space Programme (the what... ?)

What, I hear you say, of Britain's contribution to the space race? Was Dan Dare really its cutting edge? As late as 1956, Sir Richard Woolley (the Astronomer Royal, no less) told the world that space travel was 'utter bilge' (which insight earned him a leading place on the committee advising the British Government on space research). However, Britain did have a 1950s space programme. As early as 1946, the British Interplanetary Society went to the government with plans for a manned version of the V2 rocket. Their proposal predated by some fifteen years much of the technology used by the Americans in their 1961 sub-orbital space flights with astronauts Alan Shepherd and Gus Grissom, but a cash-strapped British Government could not (or would not) fund it.

The next big impetus came when Britain tested its own nuclear bomb. Having got the weapon, the government found they had no means of delivering it – their V-bombers were too vulnerable to Russian air defences (and the Russian postal system seemed a poor substitute). In 1953, they therefore commissioned aircraft maker de Havilland to produce a missile, which became the Blue Streak. This was first tested in Cumbria in August 1959, shortly before being scrapped the following April, when the powers-that-be concluded that the Russians would be able to obliterate its site before our missile had been fuelled for take -off. Meanwhile, in September 1958, Britain launched a smaller missile, the Black Knight. This, however briefly, gave Britain a lead in the space race, by achieving a world record altitude of 564km.

The two missiles went on to become parts of a multi-stage satellite launcher, the Black Prince (cancelled 1960). Blue Streak also became the first stage of a joint European carrier rocket Europa (cancelled 1972).

Britain also played an important (if unwitting) part in the Russian space programme. Russia could not supply any suitable batteries for *Sputnik*, so a member of their London diplomatic staff was sent out to buy some from a British high-street shop. They ran out after twenty-two days and *Sputnik* spent the rest of its life in silence.

And Another Thing ...

*I*n this chapter, we have a chance to include some bits of the 1950s that did not fit anywhere else in the book. In no particular order:

I'm coming out ...

In the 1950s, people did not tend to 'come out' in the modern sense of the term (not unless they wanted a criminal record). The term was used more in connection with the young ladies of a good family who became debutantes. The practice dated back to the ancient Babylonian court or, in its more modern manifestation, to the second half of the eighteenth century. By 1780, it was a well-established practice for the monarch's inner circle to return to court at the end of the hunting season. George III organised a May Ball to welcome them back, and this became an annual event and one of the highlights of the social season. This gradually evolved into a system whereby the daughters of the great and the good, at about the age of eighteen, were presented to the monarch at court and started out on a dizzying round of social events over a six month season. The presentations became huge occasions – Queen Victoria's coming out caused traffic jams along Pall Mall.

At one level, it could be seen as a very superior cattle market, at which aristocratic daughters could be advertised, in a suitably select market place, as being of marriageable age. While the young beaus were casting their lascivious eyes over the available livestock, the debs (and their mothers) would run an equally detailed measure over prospective suitors. One 1860s debutante recorded that a Mr West was worth £500 to £1,000 a year, 'But unfortunately there's madness in the family, which is rather a drawback.' Coded information would pass between families about the candidates:

FU – Financially Unsound
MTF – Must Touch Flesh
NSIT – Not Safe In Taxis
VVSITPQ – Very Very Safe In Taxis Probably Queer

(*Daily Telegraph*, 16 March 2008)

The process began with the would-be debutante applying to the monarch to be presented. Her application would require evidence of good character and the recommendation of a former debutante. If accepted, she would receive a summons (not an invitation, but a Royal command where you failed to attend at your peril) from the Lord Chamberlain. On the day, presentation meant getting dolled up according to a minutely detailed dress code (only slightly relaxed after 1939), stepping forward, curtseying and stepping back without turning one's back on the monarch – job done. This was the prelude to six months of cocktail parties, tea parties, dinners, dances and attendance at key events, such as Royal Ascot and Henley.

Why am I telling you all this in a book about the 1950s? Because 1958 was the last year in which debutantes were presented to the Queen. The world had moved on (some thought considerably before 1958) and the whole business was seen by most people as an elitist anachronism. Peter Townsend, the social editor of *The Tatler*, tried to keep the debutante industry going thereafter, but it never recovered from the loss of royal patronage and expired at about the same time as he did.

Premium bonds and the birth of Ernie

Chancellor Harold Macmillan announced a new savings scheme in his April 1956 budget. Its aim was to reduce inflation and to attract investment from those who found a flutter more attractive than earning predictable interest. Premium bonds proved immediately popular – 5 million were sold on the first day they went on the market, and £82 million had been invested by the time the first draw took place, in June 1957. In 1957, you could hold a minimum of £1 worth of bonds, a maximum of £500, and the top prize was £1,000. The Shadow Chancellor Harold Wilson thoroughly disapproved and called them 'a squalid raffle' and 'a national demoralisation', and church leaders expressed concern that the Government was creating a nation of hopeless gambling addicts.

A popular alternative name for them was Ernie bonds, after ERNIE – the Electronic Random Number Indicator Equipment used to conduct the draw. Some people evidently thought Ernie was a person, since he (it?) received Christmas cards, but it was in fact an early computer. Designed by Sydney Broadhurst, who built the wartime code-breaking Colossus machine at Bletchley Park, ERNIE was the size of a van, cost £25,000 (at 1957 prices) and could generate 2,000 random numbers an hour. This was fast enough to process the draw at the time but, by 2008, there were 40 billion bonds in the draw. If the original ERNIE were still in use today, it would take seventy-three days to make the monthly draw. We are now on to ERNIE Mark 4, which is the size of a DVD player, but can complete the process in three and a half hours.

The Great Smog of 1952

Air pollution has been a problem for as long as man has been urbanised and, in particular, has relied on coal as a fuel. As long ago as 1306, King Edward I briefly banned its use in London for this reason. From the time of the Industrial Revolution, the problem got progressively worse, as cities swelled in size and our lives were increasingly driven by steam. What happens is that the water particles that occur naturally in fogs collect around pollutants in the air, to create the yellowish smog – a term describing a mixture of smoke and fog. Some of these particles form acids, which cause skin irritation, breathing difficulties and corrode buildings. Under the right weather conditions, smog can be trapped at ground level, and without wind to move it on it can linger for days. The effects are likely to be particularly bad in the most densely developed areas and those that are low-lying and thus less windy – the East End of London and the city of Manchester were two areas that were particularly prone to smog.

There had been pressures to do something about the problem for well over a century, but they tended to founder on the economic consequences of doing so. Business interests issued dire warnings about employers being driven away by well-intentioned legislation and politicians were reluctant to impose additional costs on their voters, even if it was in the interests of their health.

Then came the great smog of December 1952. Whether this was more deadly than its nineteenth-century predecessors is a moot point, but a number of factors suggest that it might have

been. First, there were simply more people around to generate pollution. Second, post-war Britain's parlous economic state meant that our best (and least polluting) coal was reserved for export, leaving domestic users to burn the smokier varieties. Then there was the additional impact of the internal combustion engine; added to which, in London, Manchester and elsewhere, electric trams were being phased out in favour of diesel buses.

Large parts of the country were shrouded in smog for several days of almost unimaginable density and toxicity. On the Isle of Dogs, pedestrians could not even see their own feet. Cows were said to have dropped dead in the fields from breathing difficulties. Transport, even the ambulance service, ground to a halt. The fog even penetrated indoors, bringing theatre and film shows to a complete stop when customers could not see the screen or stage. Worst of all, it played havoc with people's health. An estimated 100,000 people went down with smog-related illnesses, and it is now thought that 12,000 died in the immediate aftermath of the smog, and another 8,000 in the weeks and months that followed.

Even then, the Government hesitated, because of the economic implications. (As of 1956, a ton of ordinary coal cost £8.72, whereas a ton of smokeless fuel was £10.73.) It took the findings of a Select Committee into Air Pollution and a Private Members Bill to force them into action. The Clean Air Act of 1956 created the power to declare Smoke Control Areas, in which only smokeless fuels could be burnt. This, and the move towards cleaner fuels like gas and electricity which was happening in any event, were two factors that had a dramatic impact on the quality of the air. There would still be occasional incidents of smog – December 1956 and January 1959 were two examples – but nothing on the scale of 1952.

The secret of life - revealed

On 28 February 1953, two men walked into a Cambridge pub and announced to the assembled drinkers that they had discovered the secret of life. Normally, the landlord would have been within his rights to refuse to serve them, because they'd obviously had enough, but these two happened to be James D. Watson and Francis Crick, two scientists at Cambridge University and they had done just what they said. In a learned paper, published in the journal *Nature* that April, they described the structure of deoxyribonucleic acid (DNA to the rest of us) which, they modestly observed, 'has novel features which are of considerable biological interest'.

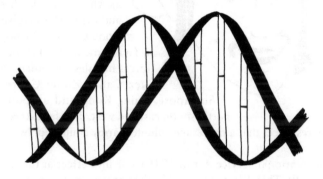

DNA is the material that makes up genes and enables living organisms to pass on inherited characteristics, and its discovery would transform whole branches of science – medicine, agriculture, computing, nanotechnology and forensics, to name but a few. Their work won them – and a third colleague, Maurice Wilkins – Nobel prizes in 1962. A fourth colleague, Rosalind Franklin, died of cancer in 1958, aged just thirty-seven, before she could receive equal recognition. (In those days, Nobel prizes were not awarded posthumously.)

Watson and Crick did not discover DNA. That was the achievement of Swiss physician Friedrich Miescher as long ago as 1869 (though he called it 'nuclein'). It was known from the 1920s to be the stuff of inheritance, but establishing its structure unlocked the secret of how genetic information is stored, transferred and copied.

The Big Call-up

After the war, Britain still harboured delusions of imperial greatness and clung to the view that we should – and, more to the point, could – take on a substantial role as the world's chief authority. This involved stationing 100,000 troops in Germany, and substantial forces in Palestine, Aden, the Suez Canal Zone, Cyprus, Singapore, Hong Kong and all points north, south, east and west. This far exceeded the resources that a peacetime volunteer army could supply.

The National Service Act of 1948 came into effect at the start of 1949. This dictated that all healthy males aged seventeen to twenty-one had to do eighteen months National Service, after which they remained on the reserve list for four years, during which time they could be recalled to their units up to three times, for periods of up to twenty days. The only ways to avoid it were:

✳ failing the medical

✳ prove yourself to be a conscientious objector, or homosexual

✳ be employed in one of the 'essential' services – coal mining, farming or the merchant navy

One further way out, which was pursued by just a handful of men, was to stand for Parliament. With the outbreak of the Korean War in 1950, the period of National Service was increased by six months, though the reserve period was reduced by a corresponding amount.

Between 1947 and May of 1963 (when the last National Serviceman – called up in December 1960 – returned to civilian life), some 2.3 million young men went through the process. Many of them saw combat and some 400 died in the course of it. Others were used as guinea pigs in atomic tests and may have suffered long-term damage to their health due to exposure to radiation. A larger number will remember the absurdities of army life: an induction period with endless square bashing; cross-country runs; route marches; physical training; preparation for gas warfare (which seemed to consist of more of the above, but in a gas mask); interspersed with menial or simply ludicrous tasks (peeling mountains of potatoes or painting the coal white) and all imposed by psychopathic sergeant majors.

Many people today believe it would be a jolly good thing to reintroduce National Service, for instance the forces' sweetheart, Dame Vera Lynn:

> All young men should have a certain time in the army, instead of running around wild for a few years after school. They would learn discipline and they would learn a good trade. It would be a good opportunity.

One group that might not welcome its reintroduction are the armed forces themselves. Their experience seems to have been that it provided many more recruits than even the armed forces needed, that the training of these took resources away from the army's core business, and that the negative experience of the armed forces that many conscripts took back into their communities actually harmed their mainstream recruitment efforts. In addition, it tended to discourage young people taking up apprenticeships immediately on leaving school, knowing that they would be interrupted part of the way through. And last but not least, there is the consideration of whether providing all young people with the skills (and the weapons) to kill, at an age when their hormonally driven homicidal urges might be expected to be at their height, is necessarily a good thing.

Red sky at night - Windscale's alight!

British scientists helped the Americans develop nuclear technology, but by the 1950s the Americans had decided not to share further developments with her allies. This meant that Britain had to become self-sufficient in weapons of mass destruction if they wanted to remain a big player in military terms. One essential ingredient of this was the fuel for atomic bombs so, in great haste and in a time of austerity, two atomic piles were built in Cumbria to manufacture plutonium. According to one of the physicists who worked on them, their design was 'dodgy' from the start. Their safety was further compromised when they were adapted to produce tritium for a more advanced bomb. In October 1957, while undergoing routine maintenance, it was noticed first that the plant was overheating, then that it was on fire.

Nobody quite knew what to do with 9 tons of uranium burning at up to 1,300 degrees centigrade. The plant was air-cooled, so first they tried turning the cooling fans up. This unsurprisingly had the effect of fanning the flames. Squirting carbon dioxide and then water on the fire was equally ineffective, and water ran the additional risk of the plant starting to manufacture hydrogen and exploding. The flames only began to subside when they cut off the supply of air to the plant.

This was at the time the world's worst nuclear accident, scoring five on a scale that only went up to seven. Pollution from it was detected as far afield as Belgium, Germany and Norway. More locally, milk produced in the area around the plant had to be heavily diluted and poured into the Irish Sea. One estimate suggests that some 240 additional cases of thyroid cancer would have resulted from the accident (though conspiracy theorists would add several noughts to that figure and shout 'cover-up').

One irony was that these plants were obsolescent and overdue for closure. Nearby Calder Hall had been producing plutonium by a safer process since August 1956. Both plants were rendered unsalvageable and none have been built to a similar design since.

A report on the causes of the accident was commissioned from a leading scientist, Sir William Penney. He completed it in 1957, but it did not enter the public realm until 1988 (and then in a much-altered form, which shifted blame onto the operatives – many of whom had shown great bravery in putting the fire out – rather than fundamental design faults). Harold Macmillan's view was that secrecy was necessary, to avoid denting confidence in the nuclear industry and prejudicing the nuclear programme.

If you enjoyed this book, you may also be interested in …

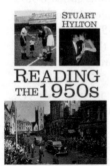

Reading: The 1950s

STUART HYLTON

In *Reading: The 1950s* Stuart Hylton gives a fascinating accoun of the town and its people during a decade of rapid and memorable change. The story begins in the drab atmosphere of the early post-war years, with their austerity and sense of shrinking empire and declining national prestige. It ends with the brash new world of the swinging sixties, which brought Tl Beatles, the miniskirt and the Mini car.

978 0 7524 9353 4

A 1950s Childhood: From Tin Baths to Bread and Dripping

PAUL FEENEY

Do you remember Pathé News? Taking the train to the seaside? Knitted bathing costumes? Then the chances are you were born in or around 1950. This delightful compendium o memories and illustrations, with chapters on games and hobbies, holidays, music, and fashion, will bring back this decade of childhood, and jog memories about all aspects of life.

978 0 7524 5011 7

A 1950s Housewife: Marriage and Homemaking in the 1950s

SHEILA HARDY

A 1950s Housewife collects heart-warming personal anecdote from women who embarked on married life during this fascinating post-war period, providing a trip down memory lane for any wife or child of the 1950s. This book will prove an eye-opener for those who now wish they had listened when their mothers attempted to tell them stories of the 'ol days', and will provide useful first-had accounts for those wi a love of all things kitsch and vintage.

978 0 7524 6989 8

Visit our website and discover thousands of other History Press books.

www.thehistorypress.co.uk